Bible
Speaks
today

the message of

HOSEA

Series editors:
Alec Motyer (OT)
John Stott (NT)
Derek Tidball (Bible Themes)

the message of

HOSEA

Love to the loveless
Revised edition

Derek Kidner

ivp
Academic
An imprint of InterVarsity Press
Downers Grove, Illinois

InterVarsity Press USA
P.O. Box 1400 | Downers Grove, IL 60515-1426, USA
ivpress.com | email@ivpress.com

Inter-Varsity Press, England
Studio 101, The Record Hall, 16–16A Baldwins Gardens | London, EC1N 7RJ, UK
ivpbooks.com | ivp@ivpbooks.com

InterVarsity Press® is the publishing division of InterVarsity Christian Fellowship/USA®. For more information, visit intervarsity.org.

Inter-Varsity Press, England, originated within the Inter-Varsity Fellowship, now the Universities and Colleges Christian Fellowship, a student movement connecting Christian Unions in universities and colleges throughout Great Britain, and a member movement of the International Fellowship of Evangelical Students.

Unless otherwise stated, Scripture quotations are from the Holy Bible, New International Version (Anglicised edition). Copyright © 1979, 1984, 2011 by Biblica. Used by permission of Hodder & Stoughton, an Hachette company. All rights reserved. 'NIV' is a registered trademark of Biblica, UK trademark number 1448790.

The exposition of chapter 14 first appeared as an article in *Themelios* 1.2 (Spring 1976) and is reprinted (with minor alterations) by permission.

Originally published under the title *Love to the Loveless*.

This edition published 2024.

Cover design: Cindy Kiple
Images: © MarkSkalny / iStock / Getty Images Plus

USA ISBN 978-1-5140-0645-0 (print) | USA ISBN 978-1-5140-0646-7 (digital)
UK ISBN 978-1-78974-433-0 (print) | UK ISBN 978-1-78359-642-3 (digital)

Typeset in Great Britain by CRB Associates, Potterhanworth, Lincolnshire

Printed in the United States of America ∞

Library of Congress Cataloging-in-Publication Data
A catalog record for this book is available from the Library of Congress.

British Library Cataloguing-in-Publication Data
A catalogue record for this book is available from the British Library.

30 29 28 27 26 25 24 | 8 7 6 5 4 3 2 1

Contents

General preface   vii

Author's preface   ix

Chief abbreviations   x

To the reader . . .   1

Part 1: A parable from life   7
A DISTRACTED FAMILY
(Hosea 1 – 3)

1. Introducing Hosea (1:1)   9
2. An ominous beginning (1:2–9)   11
3. A rift in the clouds (1:10 – 2:1)   16
4. The lovers and the Lover (2:2–23)   19
5. 'Love . . . as the LORD loves' (3:1–5)   30

Part 2: The parable spelt out   35
HOW CAN I GIVE YOU UP?
(Hosea 4 – 14)

6. A people without understanding (4:1–19)   37
7. The prospect darkens (5:1–14)   46
8. Let us press on to know the LORD (5:15 – 7:2)   51
9. Decadence (7:3–16)   57
10. Sowing the wind, reaping the whirlwind (8:1–14)   62
11. Wanderers among the nations (9:1–17)   69
12. 'Time to seek the LORD' (10:1–15)   75
13. 'How can I give you up?' (11:1–11)   82
14. Look back and learn! (11:12 – 12:14)   87
15. The unmaking of a kingdom (13:1–16)   93
16. The way home (14:1–9)   98

Addenda

Map: Assyria and the west   105
Map: The break-up of Israel   106
Chronological table   107
A bird's-eye view of the book   113

Bible Speaks today

GENERAL PREFACE

The Bible Speaks Today describes three series of expositions, based on the books of the Old and New Testaments, and on Bible themes that run through the whole of Scripture. Each series is characterized by a threefold ideal:

- to expound the biblical text with accuracy
- to relate it to contemporary life, and
- to be readable.

These books are, therefore, not 'commentaries', for the commentary seeks rather to elucidate the text than to apply it, and tends to be a work rather of reference than of literature. Nor, on the other hand, do they contain the kinds of 'sermons' that attempt to be contemporary and readable without taking Scripture seriously enough. The contributors to The Bible Speaks Today series are all united in their convictions that God still speaks through what he has spoken, and that nothing is more necessary for the life, health and growth of Christians than that they should hear what the Spirit is saying to them through his ancient – yet ever modern – Word.

ALEC MOTYER
JOHN STOTT
DEREK TIDBALL
Series editors

Author's preface

I am glad of this chance to thank the series editor and the editorial staff for the trouble they have taken in seeing this book through to the light of day.

I have a slight fear that the comments on (especially) the opening chapters of Hosea may be found a little heavy going – unlike the inspired text itself which is brilliantly alive. May I therefore suggest that any discouraged and flagging readers should turn to the 'Bird's-eye view' at the back of the book, to get their bearings and return refreshed to complete their journey with this remarkable prophet.

DEREK KIDNER

Chief abbreviations

ANET	*Ancient Near Eastern Texts* edited by J. B. Pritchard, 3rd edn 1969.
AV	Authorized (King James) Version, 1611.
BDB	*Hebrew–English Lexicon of the Old Testament* by F. Brown, S. R. Driver and C. A. Briggs, 1907.
BH	*Biblia Hebraica* edited by R. Kittel and P. Kahle, 7th edn 1951.
BHS	*Biblia Hebraica Stuttgartensia* edited by K. Elliger and W. Rudolph, 1977.
GNB	Good News Bible (Today's English Version), 1976.
Harper	*Amos and Hosea* by W. R. Harper (International Critical Commentary, T. & T. Clark), 1905.
Heb.	Hebrew.
IEJ	*Israel Exploration Journal.*
JAOS	*Journal of the American Oriental Society.*
JB	The Jerusalem Bible, 1966.
JTS	*Journal of Theological Studies.*
K-B	*Lexicon in Veteris Testamenti Libros* edited by L. Koehler and W. Baumgartner, 1953.
Knight	*Hosea* by G. A. F. Knight (Torch Bible Commentaries, SCM Press), 1960.
LXX	The Septuagint (pre-Christian Greek Version of the Old Testament).
Mays	*Hosea* by J. L. Mays (Old Testament Library, SCM Press), 1969.
mg.	margin.
MT	Masoretic Text (standard text of the Hebrew Bible).

NEB	The New English Bible, Old Testament, 1970.
NIV	New International Version, 2011.
NRSV	New Revised Standard Version, 1995.
Pusey	*The Minor Prophets* by E. B. Pusey, 1879.
RSV	American Revised Standard Version, 1952.
RV	English Revised Version, 1881.
Smith	*The Book of the Twelve Prophets* by George Adam Smith (The Expositor's Bible), 1, 7th edn 1900.
Syr.	The Peshitta (Syriac Version of the Bible).
VT	*Vetus Testamentum.*
Wolff	*Hosea* by H. W. Wolff (Biblischer Kommentar 14, 2nd edn 1965); English translation by G. Stansell (Fortress Press), 1974.

To the reader . . .

It is rather easy to grow up with a naïve idea of God – something like a child's impression of the adult world – and with a worrying conundrum about his way of doing things. The conundrum is this old one: If God is all-powerful and all-good, why does he not rid the world of evil? (The church too, for that matter.)

One of the things that Hosea does for us is to give us, with extraordinary frankness, the other side of that anomaly. God's side.

Children's ideas of their elders are puzzled ones. *They* make the rules (the children say to themselves) – there's power for you! And they have money, whatever they may say – there's freedom! What couldn't we do, we children, with all that freedom, all that power?

In this book we see things not in these simplistic terms, where situations and people are uncomplicated and power is like a magic wand. Hosea introduces us to a family which is a miniature of our world – or rather, of the most enlightened part of the world of his own day. But it is a problem family, and God compares his situation not to that of an autocrat whose orders nobody dares question, nor of a father who rejoices in an adoring wife and children, but to that of a husband whose wife has left him, and a father whose children are like strangers in his own house and are fast destroying themselves.

Where does omnipotence, where do instant solutions come into such a picture? Certainly tame acceptance is no answer to it, but no more are strong-arm tactics – unless one were content to have a slave-wife, and a family simply cowed into conformity. With relationships as subtle and sensitive as these, there are no shortcuts to mending them when they go wrong; not even for omnipotence. If we think that God could somehow wave that wand and solve the problem painlessly if he really gave his mind to it, we have only to recall the cross, that hideous instrument of torture, and the Son's prayer 'My Father, *if it is possible . . .*' (Matt. 26:39, 42, 44) for our answer.

But all this may seem somewhat theoretical and remote. So God brought it home to Hosea, at ground level and at painful length, by telling him to do the last thing a responsible prophet might expect. '*Go and marry a prostitute* – because' (if we may paraphrase it this way) 'this is exactly what I, the Lord, have married in pledging myself to all of *you*.'

And Hosea did not gather that he could simply go through a form of marriage, or alternatively that God would find him a prostitute with a heart of gold. He married a shallow, mercenary woman, the kind who might walk out on him the moment it suited her; and they started a family.

She bore him a son. After that, she had two more children, who were apparently not his. Then she left him.

She had made a fool of him; she had also made a fool of herself, for her new lover turned out to be as useless and heartless as herself, and she was soon his drudge and virtual prisoner. It was rather like the plight of the prodigal son.

But the story does not end in quite the same way as the well-known parable. In a sense it surpasses it. She makes no move (perhaps none is possible) to come home. It is Hosea, her husband, who goes to find her; and when he does, he not only has to win her back but buy her back, scraping together the price partly in cash and partly in kind. And more: it is not just an act of repossession, for God had said to him, 'Go again and *love* a woman loved by another man, an adulteress, and *love her as I, the Lord, love* the Israelites although they resort to other gods' (Hos. 3:1, NEB; my italics).

There is precious little exercise of power in such a story of the 'eternal triangle', for power alone would solve nothing. Instead, there is hurt, humiliation, waiting, personal approach and appeal, and, at last, mutual commitment. Cost, too; but mostly the cost of risking rebuff, reopening wounds, working at a difficult relationship and being determined that it shall last and grow. 'I am now going to allure her,' says God, '. . . and speak tenderly to her . . . I will betroth you to me for ever' (Hos. 2:14, 19). And Hosea, for his part, says to his wife Gomer that he is not for sharing, nor is she. 'You are to live with me for many days; you must not be a prostitute or be intimate with any man, and I will behave the same way toward you' (Hos. 3:3).

That is the story of the first three chapters. But when God draws out the large-scale meaning of it, it turns out that the pattern of relationships, between him, his people and his rivals for their affection, is not so much a triangle as a veritable polygon. In every direction his people have played him false:

- in religion, with other gods, another cult;
- in politics, with shabby intrigues and dubious patrons;
- in morals, with unbridled sex and violence.

His reaction might well have been to write them off and waste no more affection on them. But he is not so easily dismissed.

So far, I have been playing down the role of forceful intervention. But it would be a gross distortion of this book to make it portray God as simply wringing his hands. There is anger here, and judgment; it is not all pleading. At this point it may help us to see the realities of the situation and the lack of easy remedies if we glance at the troubles of our own society and the simplistic cures that are proposed for them. 'Play it cool', one school of thought will urge the legislators: let the facts of life bring people to their senses in their own time. 'Play it tough' will be another view: bring in stiffer laws and savage penalties. 'Play it tenderly' will be a third opinion: appeal to people's better feelings; trust the strong to act with moderation.

Each of these *by itself* would cut a vital corner, to leave an open path to either anarchy or civil war or a bullies' paradise. One must have, it seems, the right mix of all three of them, or more; a complex answer to a complex situation.

In Hosea, God is by turns *cool* ('he has withdrawn himself from them'; 'Ephraim is joined to idols; leave him alone!'; 'They sow the wind and reap the whirlwind'; Hos. 5:6; 4:17; 8:7) and *tough* ('I will be like a lion to Ephraim'; 'God will remember their wickedness and punish them for their sins'; Hos. 5:14; 9:9); but above all, *tender* ('How can I give you up, Ephraim? . . . My heart is changed within me'; 'I will heal their wayward-ness'; Hos. 11:8; 14:4).

And Israel? She got it wrong, in the usual human way. God, she reckoned, must be wanting more religion; she would bring more sacrifices. They love sacrifice, says God, 'when they go with their flocks and herds to seek the LORD' (Hos. 8:13; 5:6). But that was not the way to find him. These

3

were religious *things*, and he wanted people: converted people, deeply repentant, wholly and for ever his. All the ups and downs of the book, the scathing portraits, dire predictions, ardent appeals, add up to this; and the book ends by looking to the fruit of all this agony, when this unequal marriage, like Hosea's, will be no longer full of tensions and betrayals, but secure and blissful, its long winter over and its spring at last arrived and in full flower.

What, then, has this prophet to say to us today? This at least:

- that God is not the distant magician of our childish imagining (which is where we began), but one who works within the very limits and freedoms that can make or break a marriage, a family, a people or a person;
- that he loves the loveless, and values the otherwise worthless – enough to let the ransom for them cost him everything;[1]
- but equally, that he will never be content to form one side of any triangle – still less, of any polygon! – or to be the bridegroom of a day or two. He will settle for nothing less than love, nothing shorter than 'for ever'.

So, 'whoever is wise',[2] 'take with you words, and turn to the LORD', perhaps in the very language of 14:2–3 (here quoted from the AV):

say unto him, Take away all iniquity, and receive us graciously:
. . . for in thee the fatherless findeth mercy.

Then we can expect to hear from him the princely response which words from the heart, such as these, will still evoke:

I will heal their backsliding,
I will love them freely:
for mine anger is turned away.

And the poetry that follows this, although it speaks to ancient Israel, still speaks volumes to us as the dry, drab and superficial creatures that we are:

---

[1] See the comments, below, on 3:2 and 13:14.

[2] This is how the epilogue, the last verse of the book, addresses us. It is not a message simply for its own times or its first hearers.

I will be as the dew unto Israel:
he shall grow as the lily,
and cast forth his roots as Lebanon.

Such is the God who meets us, exposes us, wrestles with us, and, if we will, heals us in these chapters.

Part 1: A parable from life
A DISTRACTED FAMILY
(Hosea 1 – 3)

It is the people you love who can hurt you most. One can almost trace the degree of potential pain along a scale – from the rebuff you hardly notice from a stranger, to the rather upsetting clash you may have with a friend, right on to the stinging hurt of a jilting, the ache of a parent–child estrangement, or, most wounding of all, the betrayal of a marriage.

Nothing short of the last two of these could really have conveyed to Hosea or to us how deeply God cares about us. Even then, words alone might have failed to bring home the sharpness of it. It needed acting out, and in real life at that.

After the briefest of time notes, in the opening verse we are plunged straight into the story.

Hosea 1:1

1. Introducing Hosea

So we make acquaintance with the prophet and his times. His name has suffered a little in its journey into English via Greek and Latin (where it is called Osee), for it should be Hoshea – the name also of the last king of Israel (2 Kgs 17:1), and the name originally borne by Joshua. Like Joshua/ Jesus, it is derived from the verb 'to save'.[1]

The kings who are named here span most of the eighth century BC, but they are outshone by the brilliant prophets of that time: Jonah, Amos and Hosea in (mainly) the north, and Micah and Isaiah in the south.[2]

It had been at first a time of growing affluence, thanks to the brief respite these little kingdoms found themselves enjoying while their strongest neighbours happened, for once, to be preoccupied and weak. Damascus, their most recent scourge, had been crippled by Assyria in 802; and then Assyria itself, that grim Mesopotamian war machine, had begun to falter under threats from without and disunity within.

But with Israel's wealth had come increasing decadence; and then, halfway through the century, their world began to crumble. At home, the two strong kings, Jeroboam II of Israel and his contemporary, Uzziah of Judah, were at or near the end of their long reigns, while in the distance

---

[1] Compare Num. 13:8 (Hoshea) with 14:6 (Joshua) = Neh. 8:17, AV (Jeshua) = Acts 7:45, AV (Jesus). 'Jesus' is the Greek form of Jeshua/Joshua.

[2] North and south had split apart in the tenth century BC after the death of Solomon to form two kingdoms, existing mostly at odds with each other. The ten tribes of the north ('Israel', or 'Ephraim') had a turbulent history of coups and counter-coups, and were more exposed than the small southern kingdom ('Judah') to invasion. Judah was ruled, throughout, by a single dynasty, the house of David. For details, see the table on pp. 107ff. and the map on p. 106. The fact that Hosea mentions here no northern king after Jeroboam may indicate that, like Amos (Amos 7:12f.), he was forced to prophesy to Israel from the safety of the land of Judah in his later years.

Assyria had roused itself to a new pitch of terrifying strength and militancy. It was soon to march on Palestine. Within a generation the kingdom of Israel would be extinct.

It was to this generation that Hosea was sent to preach repentance.

Hosea 1:2–9

2. An ominous beginning

A prophet's call could be agonizing: he would know that almost anything might be asked of him. It would be hard, though, to find a more shattering first demand than was made of Hosea. The Jerusalem Bible (JB) gives it to us with almost the merciless brevity of the original: 'Go, marry a whore, and get children with a whore, for the country itself has become nothing but a whore by abandoning Yahweh' (2).

This is strong talk. And as if throwing the word 'whore' at us three times in one sentence were not enough, the Hebrew has the root not a mere three times, but four.[1]

Was it meant literally?

On the face of it, yes: exactly as it reads. Possibly, though, it may foreshorten the picture, leaping ahead to what this woman would become, as God could see. (This way of taking it is not as arbitrary as it may look, since this is evidently how the children are mentioned. They were future, as the unfolding story shows, yet the command of verse 2 runs literally 'take to yourself a wife of harlotry and children of harlotry', as though the latter already existed.)

The harsher view, that Gomer was a whore already, seems to me the right one; but whichever view we take, we should not soften it by making her a cult-prostitute, merely deluded and misused; for the Hebrew has a word for this (4:14), and it is not the word used here.[2] What Hosea had to

---

[1] The expression in v. 2 'has become nothing but a whore' (JB), or 'commits great whoredom' (NRSV), renders a Hebrew construction which uses the verbal root twice over (infinitive absolute plus imperfect) – a common way of reinforcing a statement.

[2] Still less should we allegorize it away. While the children's names were given them to convey a message, the name Gomer and her father's name Diblaim are marks of actuality, as are the statements concerning each child's conception and birth.

do was, in miniature, what God had done in giving his love to a partner with a history and with a roving eye. Hosea was not to leave the matter there, any more than God would; but that belongs to a later part of the story, told in chapter 3.

Meanwhile, in this opening phase, it is the children who must capture our attention. What they are and what they are called will be the embodiment of God's word to Israel and to us: each of them a living sign and portent.

1. The first portent: the boy Jezreel (1:3b–5)

The three portents are a crescendo – first of judgment, but in the end a crescendo of grace to round off each of the first two chapters. Grace has a way of interrupting oracles of doom (like the 'cheerfulness' which 'was always breaking in' when Dr Johnson's friend began philosophizing);[3] but for the moment there is no break in the clouds, and the darkness will get deeper with each successive birth.

Jezreel (*yizrĕʿel*) might not seem to be a particularly ominous name. In its form it was the same type of name as Israel (*yiśrāʾēl*), and although it could yield a hidden meaning, to be brought out in 2:22, it would speak in the first place of a well-known town and valley of the northern kingdom. That town, though, had seen King Jehu's bloodbath,[4] and God is showing that he has not for a moment forgotten this. For a prophet to give his son such a name was like a politician naming his child Peterloo or Katyn or Soweto. And he would miss no opportunity of explaining it.

The explanation in verse 4, which foretells retribution on the house of Jehu, goes on to include the whole kingdom; and so in fact it came about. The house of Jehu fell in about 752 BC with King Zechariah's murder (2 Kgs 15:8–12), and after thirty years of coups and counter-coups the kingdom was torn to pieces by Assyria, never to recover.

There is a paradox over Jehu. Here he is a man of blood, storing up disaster for his dynasty and realm; but in 2 Kings 10:30 he has 'done well' in carrying out against the house of Ahab 'all [God] had in mind to do'. The reason is not far to seek; it lies in Jehu himself, a standing example of a

---

[3] *Boswell's Life of Johnson* (Everyman), II, p. 218.
[4] The gruesome story is told in 2 Kgs 9 and 10. For Jehu's place among the kings of Israel, see the table of kings on p. 107.

human scourge. As God's executioner he left nothing undone, and it was in that capacity that he collected his reward: the promise of the throne to four generations of his sons. The Old Testament has several instances of this kind of servant, of whom Sennacherib, whom God calls 'the rod of my anger' ('But this is not what he intends, this is not what he has in mind', Isa. 10:7), and Nebuchadnezzar 'my servant' (Jer. 27:6) are prime examples. And they were paid their wages – paid in spoil and conquest, described in exactly these terms of 'wages' in Ezekiel 29:18–20; but paid also with the due requital of their pride and cruelty (see, e.g., Isa. 10:12, 15ff.; Isa. 47; Dan. 4).

So it was with Jehu – with the difference that he knew of his commission from the Lord. But there was no difference of spirit or method. The events of 2 Kings 10 are a welter of trickery, butchery and hypocrisy, in which the only trace of a religious motive is fanaticism – and even this is suspect in view of Jehu's charade of sacrificing to Baal (2 Kgs 10:25). Self-interest and bloodlust were his dominant springs of conduct, and it was this that made 'the blood of Jezreel' an accusing stain.

If we ask why Israel, a hundred years later, should have to suffer for this, the later chapters of the book will reply that neither Israel nor her royal house ever repudiated this attitude to violence. Jezreel was only one episode of a continuous story (cf., e.g., 4:1–3; 7:1–7), and God could be no party to it.

There is a double sting in the tail of this brief oracle. Usually when God promises to 'break the bow' of some fighting force, it means that he is coming to his people's rescue. There is a notable example in 2:18, and another in Psalm 46:9. But here, pointedly, it is the bow of *Israel* that he will break. As a kingdom, it is no longer a force for God, if it ever has been. To keep it intact would be an unreality. The further sting of this final sentence is the great reversal it implies by the scene of the defeat. Jezreel, the valley of Gideon's victory (Judg. 6:33 – 7:23), had been a name once covered with glory. Now, since the massacres, it could only stand for savagery.

So it turned out. In 733, a decade before the death of the kingdom as a whole, an Assyrian army fought its way into this valley and lopped off the northern territories of Israel, marching their inhabitants off to Assyria. In 2 Kings 15:29 'Gilead and Galilee'. God had broken the bow of Israel, and it lay defenceless.[5]

---

[5] See the map on p. 106.

2. The second portent: the girl 'Not Pitied' (1:6–7)

The first child had been Hosea's own: his wife 'bore him a son' (3). The second and third are not said to have been his: the 'him' of verse 3 is missing in verses 6 and 8. So the joy of fatherhood was deeply clouded, and the children were living proofs of the invasion of the marriage.

The name *Lo-Ruhamah*, 'Not loved' or 'Not pitied', uses the same verb (but a different part of it)[6] as in the well-known saying of Isaiah 49:15, 'Can a mother forget the baby at her breast, *and have no compassion . . .* ?' The effect of the name is startling and tragic: the sign cuts deeper than the first one, Jezreel, for while it is shattering enough to lose a war and a kingdom, it is still more desperate to lose the mercy and compassion of God. We must not press the distinction too far, for this book above all reveals the persistence of God's compassion, even in this opening chapter and still more towards the closing pages (see especially Hos. 11). But his love is not blind, nor is it coercive. It follows that since mercy without response is self-defeating, and forgiveness without a healed relationship is empty, there may come a point at which the only thing left for even God to say is, 'How often I have . . . and you were not willing. Look, your house is left to you desolate' (Matt. 23:37–38).

The verse about Judah (7) underlines the fact that, in this context, pity or the lack of it means not a state of mind but a course of action, sparing or unsparing. God's *love to Judah* would take the form of a miraculous deliverance, the rescue of Jerusalem after Hezekiah had spread the Assyrian ultimatum before the Lord (Isa. 37:14, 33ff.).[7] There would be no such reprieve for an impenitent Samaria.[8] Pity in that form would only prolong the process of its dying.

It needs to be said, as well, that oracles like these are shouts of warning, not irrevocable sentences. The classic illustrations of this fact are found in Jonah and Jeremiah. Jonah's oracle, 'Forty more days and Nineveh will be overthrown' (Jon. 3:4), was as doom-laden as even he could wish; yet he knew that it was given to avert the very judgment it foretold. Jeremiah had

---

[6] Strictly speaking, the name is a statement: 'She has not received compassion.' Cf. 2:1 (3, Heb.); 1 Pet. 2:10.

[7] Those who cannot entertain the idea of prediction treat verse 7 as an insertion after the event. But it has an important function in the oracle as a provocative challenge to Israel. 'This', God says in effect, 'is the salvation in store for your sister kingdom. This is what your impenitence is forfeiting.'

[8] See the information on p. 97.

the principle spelt out to him in the potter's workshop, as he saw the craftsman's response, radical and creative, to the way his material responded or failed to respond to him. God's comment was far-reaching: 'If at any time I announce that a nation . . . is to be uprooted, torn down and destroyed, and if that nation . . . repents of its evil, then I will relent and not inflict on it the disaster I had planned' (Jer. 18:7–8). This principle of all prophecy (note the words 'at any time') throws its own light on the way the chapter will end. But before that there is worse to come.

3. The third portent: the boy 'Not My People' (1:8–9)

This son, *Lo-Ammi*, like his sister (see on verse 6), seems to have been a product of Gomer's 'whoredom', as verse 2 puts it (see NRSV). Whether spoken or unspoken, the words 'you are not my child' must have formed themselves in the mind many times as Hosea contemplated the boy. To him as to us, the pathos of his situation could hardly fail to sensitize him to the profound sadness of the words to Israel: *you are not my people, and I am not your God*[9] – words which might otherwise have sounded only unfeeling and dismissive.

From one angle this oracle was simply factual: just as accurate as would have been Hosea's disclaimer of paternity for his children. Israel might be nominally the Lord's, but in fact she was the child of her times and of her pagan world. Likewise Yahweh might be nominally her national God; but since he is not for sharing, the presence of other gods flatly denied the relationship.

---

[9] More accurately, 'and I am not yours'. The wording of the Heb. may be meant to recall the 'I AM' passage of Exod. 3 by the contrast with Exod. 3:12, 'I am [or 'will be'] with you.'

Hosea 1:10 – 2:1

3. A rift in the clouds

This is astounding. Here are three disastrous oracles utterly reversed, and a promise of family reunion thrown in for good measure. But the about-turn will in fact be Israel's, not God's. The mention of *the sand on the seashore, which cannot be measured or counted*, takes us back to Abraham, to remind us that the ancient promise is still there, and God still holds to it. One way or another – and the New Testament has surprises in store about this – he will see it through into reality.

Two of the many statements of this old promise are in fact alluded to in verse 10 (Gen. 22:17; 13:16, respectively), for God reiterated it to Abraham, and varied the analogy by speaking of stars, sand and the dust of the earth to make the matter vivid. Isaiah would have to strike a warning note about this multitude, to show that something more than simple population growth was meant: that first there must be a sifting that would leave the merest remnant of true converts (Isa. 10:20–23). Hosea has already spoken of this coming ordeal, and it forms the background to the promise.

The heart of this good news is reconciliation. The *great . . . day of Jezreel* (11) must await explanation till 2:21–23, but the giving of new names (2:1) by an act of pure grace (like that of the Christian gospel) exactly cancels the existing alienation;[1] and the warmth of 1:10b has already gone still further, exchanging terms of covenant for those of the family: *children of*

---

[1] As reflected in NIV, in 2:1 (3, Heb.) the Heb. text has the plural 'your brothers . . . your sisters'. By attaching the plural ending (here the letter *m*) to the beginning of the words that follow these, one can get near to the singular ('brother . . . sister'), which NRSV adopts from LXX; but the plural is just as likely to be right, since the oracle is meant for all who constitute the people of Israel.

the living God. The mood is that of the great parable, as though to say, 'These sons of mine were dead and are alive again; they were lost and are found' (cf. Luke 15:24).

In terms of Old Testament Israel, the natural context is the coming exile and scattering, implied by the reversal in verse 11 when this speaks of their being gathered together and going up from the land (presumably of their captivity).[2] The other abnormality in their situation was their long-standing breach with Judah (11); and this too would be ended.

There was some degree of fulfilment of these things at the literal level – but only some. The northern kingdom ('Israel' or 'Ephraim', as distinct from Judah) never regained its cohesion after 722 BC when it was crushed and scattered. But remnants of it took refuge with Judah, and although King Hezekiah's overtures to the northern tribes were scorned at first, we read of elements from at least five of them which joined him at Jerusalem for his great Passover (2 Chr. 30:11, 18). The concept of a single people of God was far from dead. In the next century King Josiah of Judah reckoned to include the whole land of Israel in his reforms (2 Chr. 34:6–7, 9; cf. 35:18); and after the exile we read of people from Ephraim and Manasseh (1 Chr. 9:3) – which may be a term for the northern tribes in general – settling in Jerusalem with the people of Judah, Benjamin and Levi, the tribes which from then on formed the main body of Israel. Although 'Judah' and 'Jews' became their national name, the title that still meant most to them was 'Israel', whose tradition of twelve tribes now stood for the chosen nation in its completeness rather than its diversity.

So Ezra and his band of pilgrims from Babylonia offered 'twelve bulls for all Israel' when they reached Jerusalem (Ezra 8:35); and Paul, long after, spoke to Agrippa of 'our twelve tribes' waiting for the hope of Israel (Acts 26:7) – to take just one New Testament example. At this level, then, the old breach between south and north had long been healed by New Testament times, though hardly in the way that might have been foreseen, and not without new roots of bitterness in the hatred between Jews and Samaritans.

But we are not allowed to stop there. Twice the New Testament picks up this prophecy and turns it to face a still larger multitude, to include now

---

[2] It has been suggested that *land* is a scribal error for 'lands'. This would make good sense and agree with other prophecies (e.g. Jer. 16:15), but it lacks textual support and must remain a conjecture.

Samaritans and Gentiles, to whom God was saying with even better reason:

> I will call them 'my people' who are not my people;
> and I will call her 'my loved one' who is not my loved one.[3]

And this was no afterthought. As Paul reminds us, it was part of the basic promise to Abraham. 'Scripture', he points out, 'foresaw that God would justify the Gentiles by faith, and announced the gospel in advance to Abraham: "All nations will be blessed through you." So', he adds, 'those who rely on faith are blessed along with Abraham, the man of faith' (Gal. 3:8–9; cf. Rom. 4:9–25).

The prophecy, in fact, after touching down in the post-exilic age, leaps into the present and names us who are believers 'the Israel of God', whether we are Jews or Gentiles. Such is the New Testament's unfolding of the oracle; and such a consummation was the joy that drew Jesus to the cross, to 'die . . . not only for that nation but also for the scattered children of God, to bring them together and make them one' (John 11:51–52; cf. our verse 11).

---

[3] See Rom. 9:25–26; cf. 1 Pet. 2:10ff.

Hosea 2:2–23

4. The lovers and the Lover

The delightful ending of chapter 1 was totally unexpected, the surprise of it highlighting the sheer grace of God it reveals. Now in chapter 2 we move to the same climax, with an ending that is richly happy; but we see the divine Lover taking his time and using every art to win a response that will make the reconciliation genuine.

1. She is not for sharing (2:2–4)

The focus shifts now from the children to the mother, and for a little while the whole family is in view together. But as materials for God's analogy they will mostly have to play their separate parts. From one angle, Israel in her apostasy could be compared to a brood of children out of control (Jezreel, 1:4) or born out of wedlock (1:6–9), but from another angle Israel is like a fickle wife. The second of these will be the main theme of our chapter; but at its beginning and end the children make a brief but memorable appearance. Insofar as they stand for a separate entity within Israel, they are perhaps the actual hearers over against the corporate Israel whose history has made them what they are.

We can get a slightly false impression from the opening cry *Rebuke . . . rebuke*, for it means the kind of pleading or contending that belongs to a court of law. So NEB puts it well with 'Plead my cause'. It is in fact essentially the same word as in 4:1 where the Lord has 'a charge to bring' against the inhabitants of the land. NEB may well be right, too, in framing the next two lines as a question: 'Is she not my wife and I her husband?' – for the whole thrust of the book is that God will not go back on the marriage vows he has exchanged with her.[1] If not a question, it must be taken existentially, to mean 'She is no longer a wife to me' (GNB) – in other words, 'the reality has gone out of the relationship'.

Now, still in verse 2, comes the first of many calls to radical repentance – for it will keep emerging that Israel, like most of us, is readier to say she is sorry than to make a clean break with her way of life. And with the next two verses (3–4) comes the sharp reminder that this deserted husband is no pathetic cuckold but very much a person to be reckoned with. There is poetic justice in the threat to *strip her naked*, for it is in one sense a saturation dose of her own medicine, cheapening her, as in verse 10, even beyond her own self-cheapening; and in another sense it speaks of stark destitution – as the desert scene of verse 3b makes plain. Hosea's own wife was to know something of both these things, degradation and want; but God is talking about Israel and her spiritual adultery, her godless progeny (verse 4, taking us back to 1:6) and her coming devastation.

2. The rude awakening (2:5–13)

Sexual lust can be glamourized – almost canonized – by any number of attractive names, but not everyone cares to be known for setting a price on their favours. This particular charmer is allowed no aura of romanticism. She has 'played the whore' (5, NRSV), for a harlot's *pay* (12). Her lovers are many but her motive is one – the reward she can earn. The bulk of this chapter therefore deals with her on this level, only coming to anything deeper towards the end.

In this way as in others it has common ground with the story of the prodigal son, who came home not for love but because (as our verse 7 puts it) *then I was better off than now*. The love – at least initially – was all on the other side.

The prosaic facts behind the poetry of verse 5 (which would have been self-evident to those who heard it first) are that the gods of Canaan were largely patrons of fertility. To get the best results of farming one would be tempted to enlist their help, imagining that Yahweh must be somewhat out of his depth in such a realm. (*She has not acknowledged*, the Lord

---

[1] There is a similar scouting of such a thought in Isa. 50:1, where God treats the idea of divorce as no less preposterous than the notion that he might have had to sell her to pay his bills! He goes on to say that Israel did have to be 'sold' and 'sent away' (i.e. into exile) for her sins; but he has already made it clear that this was, in C. R. North's phrase, 'separation, not divorce'.

exclaims, *that I was the one who gave her the grain, the new wine and oil*, 8.) More than that, these gods were Baals, meaning lords or husbands, and while some of their rituals were a re-enacting of their wars and victories, or of vegetation's death and resurrection, which would supposedly ensure the progress of the seasons and the crops, other rituals were sexual acts with cultic prostitutes, whereby the coitus at the sanctuary would magically induce fertility in the flocks and herds and farm produce.

These beliefs and half-beliefs are not as foreign or remote from our age as they may seem. The idea that the Lord God has little relevance to the natural world is taken for granted by our secularized majority, and can be a hidden influence on even the minority who would consciously reject it. Whether his place is taken by a rational construct such as 'nature' or by the fantasies of astrology or by recourse to the occult and the demonic, it amounts to a modern dethroning of God which is hardly different from his displacement by the Baals. And this is not the only similarity between our age and theirs. If sex was deified in polytheistic thought, it receives almost equal adulation in our own. The crude pagan symbols of fertility, the likening of El or Baal to a bull,[2] the sexual acts at the sanctuary – these were not pointless pornography but expressions of a belief that this kind of potency and fecundity is what life and the world itself are chiefly about. But with it there was the fascination of the forbidden and decadent – the exciting exchange of Yahweh's broad daylight for the twilight world of violent gods, with their raw passions, cruelties and ecstasies; an exchange which has a perennial appeal.

We can note a further link with the present in the trend of Israel towards religious syncretism (that is, the mixing and merging of one religion with another); but this will be discussed in the comments on verses 16 and 17.

Returning to the text of verses 5–13 we find God speeding the process of disillusion – for such it is. The 'lovers', the pagan gods and their equivalents, are illusions that recede with every step one takes towards them; but in times of plenty this unreality is not very evident. It takes the *thornbushes* and the blank *wall* (6) of famine and frustration to dash one's hopes of them ('Where then are the gods you made for yourselves? Let them come if they can save you'; Jer. 2:28).[3] Even then one may not come

---

[2] E.g. in *ANET*, pp. 139a, 142, where the emphasis is on sexual prowess.

[3] The chapter in Jeremiah develops the theme of the unfaithful wife with considerable poetic resource.

to one's senses like the prodigal or like the truant wife who is hopefully depicted in verse 7b, but curse God like the people of Isaiah 8:21.

How wilful was Israel's ignorance (8) in chasing these lovers? JB (cf. GNB) makes it quite deliberate: 'She would not acknowledge, not she, that I was the one . . .' But while this would reinforce the blame that God puts on her, the fundamental charge against her is unfaithfulness to which her lovers' promises have lured her, as it seems from verses 5–7. So the simple translation 'she did not [or 'does not'] know'[4] seems the truer to the context while still allowing us to comment, 'But she ought to have known!'

In her sin against love there is a further twist of her knife at the end of verse 8, where she has not only ignored the true Giver but has heaped gifts on his usurper. Once more (we can note in passing) the readers may find themselves confronted by a mirror rather than a window, since Israel's sin is also humanity's and every individual's.

The punishment of verses 9–13 is unsparing, yet not unjust; in fact, as the sequel will show in 14ff., it is far from unfeeling. It is a bitter lesson, but at all costs it must be learnt. In this presentation of it the literal and the metaphorical are intertwined but easily distinguished. There is a bleak prospect of failed harvests and of farms and orchards reverting to the wild (strongly implying in 12b a depopulated land, its inhabitants deported or decimated); and behind it there is the failed promise of the Baals, for whom an infatuated Israel had dolled herself up, flirting with them at the very feasts (11) which were given to cement her union with the Lord.

But the Lord keeps the initiative, not only in judgment but in grace. Suddenly the whole scene lights up.

3. The constant Lover (2:14–17)

There is a right infatuation (implied in the Hebrew for *allure her*, 14) as well as a disastrous one, for true love need be no less ravishing than false: only less disappointing. The Lord now for his part[5] will exert his charms and speak to the heart[6] of his beloved. This is the positive and creative

---

[4] 'Know' is the primary sense of this verb, which turns into 'acknowledge' when followed by a noun or pronoun in some contexts: e.g. Jer. 3:13; Prov. 3:6.

[5] The *I* of verse 14 is emphatic.

[6] This is the Heb. idiom for *speak tenderly*. It is used in contexts of wooing (Gen. 34:3), comforting (Isa. 40:2), reassuring (Gen. 50:21), winning round (Judg. 19:3) and showing kindness (Ruth 2:13).

side of his severity, for *the wilderness* could mean one of two things for Israel: either her life in ruins, or her pilgrim spirit and youthful promise recaptured. Here it offers her the second, by way of the first. The thought of setting out with God is picked up by a later prophet, who sang of that short-lived honeymoon:

> I remember the devotion of your youth,
>> how as a bride you loved me
> and followed me through the wilderness,
>> through a land not sown.
> (Jer. 2:2)

So now, out of disaster and exile the Lord plans to create as fruitful a new era as that which the exodus had promised to bring in. What has been lost in judgment can be restored in mercy – the ruined vines of verse 12 answered by the vineyards of 15 – and what had spoilt the first victorious progress need not mar the second. That old reproach, the Valley of Achor at the gateway of the Promised Land (that is, the Valley of Trouble and of Achan's sin; Josh. 7:26), can be not just forgotten but renamed: the Door or Gate of Hope – for when God forgives, he does it handsomely, and in this single line of verse 15 he lays the ghosts of not only Israel's past but, by analogy, the past of any repentant sinner.

But salvation is not all vineyards and victories, even in the Old Testament, but at its heart the union of God and humanity. So in verses 15b–17 we are shown the answer God is waiting for, and his concern that it will mean no less than it professes. The confusion at the root of popular religion (which happily mixes one god with another, and faith with superstition) had been made still worse by the existence of the misleading word 'Baal'. In itself it simply meant 'lord', 'owner' or 'husband', and in early Israel it was sometimes used quite innocently of God, as certain personal names confirm.[7] But in Canaanite religion it stood for the most active god in the pantheon, and for his various other selves and colleagues, the god of each particular place. It was he, as divine husband, who gave the land its fertility through the rites, sexual and otherwise, performed

---

[7] Notably Beeliada ('the Lord knows'), a son of David (1 Chr. 14:7), who was also known less controversially as Eliada ('God knows') (2 Sam. 5:16). Jonathan, another loyal Yahwist, called his son Merib-Baal (1 Chr. 8:34), but 'Baal' later became regularly changed to 'Bosheth' ('shame'), and Merib-Baal has become better known to us as Mephibosheth (whose identity is confirmed by 2 Sam. 9:12).

'on every high hill and under every spreading tree', as Jeremiah 2:20 sweepingly expresses it.

This, then, had been the stain that had spread through Israel wherever the name of Baal painted a pagan image on the name of Yahweh, and brought pagan rites to his pure worship.

So it is a bold and creative stroke by which God, instead of banning sexual imagery from religion, rescues and raises it to portray the ardent love and fidelity which are the essence of his covenant. Having made this clear, he can now go on to show what concord and delight the full flowering of that marriage of God and humanity will bring.

4. Perfect bliss (2:18–20)

That day (16, 18, 21) points us on, in the Old Testament, to the great day, the Day of the Lord, not simply to a time in the near future. To us that day has dawned already in the First Advent, though it will not reach high noon until the Second.

For all its brevity, this little prophecy entwines together strands which only separately delight us in other, more familiar passages. In a few lines we have the picture of nature at peace with humanity (cf. Isa. 11:6–9; 65:25), of weapons discarded (cf. Ps. 46:9; Isa. 9:5; Mic. 4:3) and of God's people at one with him (cf. Jer. 31:33–34; Ezek. 36:26ff.). It is the last of these that God lingers over, for it is the heart of the matter.

Coming three times in quick succession, the word *betroth* gives a note of eagerness and warmth to what is promised. It makes it a new beginning, with all the freshness of first love, rather than the weary patching up of differences – and this is appropriate, since the new covenant brings with it new life. Betrothal also goes further than the courtship of verse 14, speaking of a step that was even more decisive in Israelite custom than engagement is with us. It involved handing over the bride-price to the girl's father, whose acceptance of it finalized the matter. David's betrothal to Saul's daughter, at the barbarous price demanded of him, is described in 2 Samuel 3:14 in terms which, in Hebrew, show that the five qualities listed here, ranging from *righteousness* to *faithfulness*, are thought of as the bride-price which God, the suitor, brings with him. The metaphor, of course, is imperfect, like the ransom metaphor of Mark 10:45, since there is no 'father of the bride' to receive the gift. But even in literal betrothals such a present could be passed to the bride herself to be her dowry,[8] and certainly she is the beneficiary here.

So the promise overflows with generosity. It is all of grace, and it clothes the new covenant in wedding garb. It makes three things very plain: the permanence of this union (19a), the intimacy of it (20b), and the fact that it owes everything to God.

But what exactly is this betrothal gift, leaving metaphor aside? Are these the qualities God will bring to his side of the marriage, or those that he will implant in us, his people?

The answer is surely both. Righteousness, love and the rest are pre-eminently the very stamp and character of God, and it was the lack of them on Israel's side, not on his, that had wrecked the marriage in the first place. So God's gift is that he will not only be to us all these things but will impart them, so that his bride will be no longer in fundamental discord with him and at odds with herself. It is another way of saying that he will put his law within his people and write it on their hearts (cf. Jer. 31:33).

Unwrapping, so to speak, the fivefold gift, we find first that in the Bible *righteousness* (Heb. ṣedeq) is a warmer and more positive thing than we might have dared to hope. Far from being a cold rectitude preoccupied with keeping its hands clean, true righteousness is active and generous, whether it is seen in God or men and women (cf., e.g., Ps. 111:3 with 112:9). 'Its meaning', as Norman Snaith has pointed out,[9] 'has to be found in the nature of God rather than in customs and speculations of man, however noble and splendid these thoughts and ideals may be at their best.' God's righteousness is creative, stepping in to put the very worst things right. It is so often paired with 'salvation' that some modern versions, including NRSV, tend to call it 'deliverance' or 'vindication' (e.g. Isa. 51:5–8; Ps. 98:2); and if this sometimes obscures a large part of its meaning, it captures another important part.

So, in every sense, righteousness is a gift from God; and never more so than when it means his bestowing of acceptance and acquittal on us; or in Paul's expression, 'justification'. Paul found this 'gift of righteousness' already discernible in the Old Testament (Rom. 4) and now plainly ours to 'receive', by faith in Christ (Rom. 5:17).

---

[8] Cf. Harper, p. 243, who refers to Gen. 31:15, where Laban has characteristically failed to part with it. Note also the gifts directly given to Rebekah in Gen. 24:53.

[9] N. H. Snaith, *Mercy and Sacrifice* (SCM Press, 1953), p. 76.

The second facet of the betrothal gift is *justice* (Heb. *mišpāṭ*); and this too must have its roots in God and its fruits displayed in us. At bottom it means the rulings of a judge, and while a human judge may be shallow and unfair, God's justice is 'like the depths of the sea' (Ps. 36:6, GNB), vast, profound and inexhaustible in wisdom, whether he is pronouncing a verdict or revealing his will for us – that proper ordering of life which human beings, unlike their fellow creatures, regularly disregard.

> Even the stork in the sky
> > knows her appointed seasons;
> and the dove, the swift and the thrush
> > observe the time of their migration.
> But my people do not know
> > the requirements[10] of the LORD.
> (Jer. 8:7)

The prophets found that religious people are all too happy to combine sacred rites with social wrongs; and if there is one thing that God cannot stand, this is it. Amos puts it most pungently of all:

> I hate, I despise your religious festivals;
> > your assemblies . . .
> Away with the noise of your songs . . .
> But let justice roll on like a river,
> > righteousness like a never-failing stream!
> (Amos 5:21–24)

But it is here in Hosea that justice and righteousness are seen not only as the Lord's demands but as his gifts – certainly to be worked on and cultivated, but gifts none the less.

The third facet, *love* (Heb. *ḥesed*), could be called 'devotion' or 'true love'. The older versions called it either 'mercy' or, beautifully, 'lovingkindness'; but an essential part of it is the tacit recognition of an existing bond between the parties it embraces. It implies the love and loyalty which partners in marriage or in covenant owe to one another; so it has a special relevance to what Hosea had been denied by Gomer. God

---

[10] Lit. 'judgment', i.e. *mišpāṭ*, the word we are discussing.

names it in 6:6 as the thing he most desires to see in us (see, e.g., NRSV). For God's people it sets a standard of mutual kindness and concern among themselves; but it goes further, for in 6:4 it means the love and constancy they owe to God and have so far failed to give him. As God's bridal gift, then, while it is first and foremost his devoted love towards his partner, we may see it also as the very response he intends to create in her.

The fourth word, *compassion* (Heb. *raḥămîm*), is the warmest of all terms for mercy, rather like the heartfelt compassion found in the parables and personal reactions of Jesus. It has a special link with the name of the child Lo-Ruhamah, 'Not Pitied' (1:6), which is formed from the same root. True to his nature, God could not wait to cancel that appalling name. He did so as far back as 2:1; and now, speaking to Israel as his betrothed, he makes assurance doubly sure.

But once again the dowry cannot make the marriage, unless it can also work an inward miracle. The people seen in chapter 4, who 'break all bounds . . . bloodshed follows bloodshed' (4:2), will treat compassion only as weakness, unless they are given a heart for it themselves. A later prophet, Zechariah, showed just what they had thought of 'true justice . . . mercy and compassion', using three of the very terms that come together in our verse (Zech. 7:9ff., Heb.). The 'heart of stone' would never warm towards God or people. So the gentlest of God's gifts is in some ways the most searching.

Finally, *faithfulness* (Heb. *'ĕmûnâ*). Of all qualities, this is the one most clearly lacking in a partner who has quitted. Other faults may put a marriage under strain; this one is decisive. God, of course, had been faithful all along, under endless provocation; therefore once again the betrothal gift must be not only what he himself displays but what he will implant and cultivate within his partner.

The second line of verse 20 sums up his gift: *and you will acknowledge the Lord*. This is one of the crowning promises of the new covenant (Jer. 31:34), for true knowledge depends on true likeness, and to promise the one is to promise the other. The assurance that 'we shall see him as he is' turns out to contain the unimaginable prospect that 'we shall be like him' (1 John 3:2).

5. Abundant concord (2:21–23)

The picture that we saw in verse 3 of the land under judgment, parched and crying out for relief, may help us to appreciate this sequence of petitions and answers. Tracing it backwards from verse 22b we see certain links in the chain of survival: the people (*Jezreel* – see below) looking to their crops, the crops to the soil, the soil to the sky for rain, the sky to the Lord – and *in that day*, the Day of the Lord,[11] the answer will be an abundant 'Yes!' But in fact the sequence is not traced backwards, but in its proper order beginning with the Lord. And there is more to it than a simple promise of better times to come, for it is an answer also to the labyrinthine world of polytheism, with its one god for corn, one for rain, and so on, which had stolen Israel's heart and had muddled all her thinking. Instead of that tangle of competing powers we see the one Lord from whom all blessings flow, and glimpse the orderly variety of his creation, through which his gifts are mediated not at random but within his perfect will, and not by means of magic but within a created system that makes sense and therefore can be studied and put to use. As H. W. Wolff has pointed out,

> the background of these verses indicates a genuine scientific representation of relationships within nature . . . In the book of Hosea, it is instructive to note how Israel's liberation from the nature myths of the cult of Baal permitted the free study of nature to flourish (cf. Gen. 1).[12]

It is worth adding that, however elementary and obvious this model of the natural world may seem, it is elementary in the best sense, for it brings us down to a basic presupposition from which almost every advance in practical knowledge stems: that the world is a single, close-knit composition, intelligible in principle. And it does not make the blunder of exalting that system by denying its fount and origin. So we are not left with a mechanistic world on the one hand, nor with a God who keeps us guessing on the other, but with a world we can explore and a God we can trust and serve responsibly within it.

The climax of this set of promises dispels the last shadow of the oracles of chapter 1. Already this has been anticipated in 1:10 – 2:1; now it is reiterated, and one new thing stands out at once. While the names of Hosea's second and third children ('Not Pitied' and 'Not My People') are again set free from their negatives, as in 2:1, the name of the eldest, *Jezreel*,

---

[11] See the opening comment on 2:18–20.
[12] Wolff, pp. 55f.

is now reinterpreted. Instead of being a reminder of Jehu and his massacres (see on 1:4), the name will now take its colour from the meaning of its two Hebrew components. The Hebrew *yizrĕʿel* (Jezreel) means 'God will sow', or 'May God sow'; and God now turns this into a promise that his land, long ruined and deserted, will be sown with inhabitants again. He adds, in passing, that this is *for myself* – for God, like any farmer who takes a pride in what he cultivates, hates to see his beloved land lying useless and his people scattered. His good name is bound up with all this, and for his own sake he will see the situation changed. Ezekiel 36:22ff. takes up the theme, and shows that while this approach may not be flattering it is highly reassuring, for it bases everything on God's honour, nothing on our dubious merits.

There is one other new thing. Where the earlier promise showed God saying affectionate things to Israel, such as 'children of the living God' and 'My people' (1:10; 2:1), the last words of our chapter bring back a human reply to him: *You are my God*. Like an exchange of marriage vows this mutual affirmation, 'you are mine', was the very heart of the covenant, and still is.

This brings us to the point where we are no longer overhearing a conversation between God and ancient Israel, but finding ourselves involved directly. Twice in the New Testament this 'welcome home' to those who were 'Not pitied' and 'Not my people' is quoted from our two chapters (1:10 – 2:1; 2:23) as God's word now to 'us, whom he also called, not only from the Jews but also from the Gentiles'. Paul cites it to demonstrate the unfettered grace of God towards the undeserving (Rom. 9:23–26); and Peter, to show that in Christ we are not only reconciled but incorporated into 'a chosen people . . . God's special possession' (1 Pet. 2:9–10). If this chapter therefore leaves us only contemplating God's way with ten tribes whose kingdom disappeared 2,700 years ago, we have parted company with the New Testament as well as the Old. These things constitute 'the grace', as 1 Peter 1:10 puts it, 'that was to come to you'.

Hosea 3:1–5

5. 'Love . . . as the LORD loves'

Now Hosea rounds off his own story in the first person. He uses no rhetoric. The humiliating domestic episode is recounted quietly, factually, and its bigger counterpart and prototype explained with equal objectivity. There could be no better prelude than this story to the impassioned chapters that will follow, for it shows us at the outset, as it showed Hosea, the poignant personal demands that are involved in mending any close relationship. This was no arm's-length settling of a legal battle or extracting of apologies. A marriage asks, because it offers, nothing facile or transitory; and God will be offering and asking in the coming chapters only what is from the heart and for all time.

1. The hard way home (3:1–3)

It would have been impressive enough had Hosea found that in spite of everything he still loved his truant wife, and had then perceived that God's love must be like that too. But in fact it was the other way about. It was God's love that rekindled Hosea's, when the Lord said, 'Go, love your wife again',[1] and gave him the pattern to reproduce.

There was no glossing over the unpleasant truth. The *again* in God's command faced the fact that old wounds would have to be reopened and that what had happened once might happen yet again. Also, the adultery,

---

[1] There is no ground for rendering this 'Go, *show* your love . . .' (NIV; my italics). The Hebrew has the simple imperative 'love', carrying no suggestion that love was already there, merely awaiting an outlet.

God reminded him, was still in progress:[2] it had been no isolated lapse but a desertion which added a continuing insult to the injury. The love that was asked of him would be heroic – but that was the point, for it was to be God's love in miniature.

Perhaps this is why Hosea captures, as no other writer does, the tension within God's love for his elect – for he refuses to ease the pain of the relationship either by compromise or by quitting. He loves these people despite their blatant unfaithfulness (*they turn to other gods*), which he cannot for a moment condone, and despite their fatuous and brutish scale of values. Four times this opening verse has spoken in terms of love, each pair of its occurrences placing a noble use of the word in grating proximity to a base one – pure devotion next to gross infatuation. As for the second pair, it ends in utter bathos, with God loving Israel to the uttermost, while Israel gives her heart to (of all things!) *raisin cakes*. However one may try to soften the jolt of this, by associating these delicacies with religious feasts or rare occasions,[3] the incongruity of it is still outrageous. The bride, it seems, is only here, or anywhere else, for the cakes and ale.

Screwtape, we may suppose, would have hailed this as an unusually satisfying victory for his department – for a victory it would still have been, even if the bait had had to be the world itself (cf. Mark 8:36). But (to quote that artist in temptation) 'an ever increasing craving for an ever diminishing pleasure is the formula. It is more certain; and it's better *style*. To get the man's soul and give him *nothing* in return – that is what really gladdens our Father's heart'[4] – 'our Father', of course, being Screwtape's term for the father of lies and liars. Few of us, remembering the trivialities we chase, will feel ready to cast the first stone at Israel.

So I bought her . . . The reticence is eloquent. In the single word *bought* we learn how far she had fallen, how tightly she was held, and what was the first step Hosea must take to fulfil the command to love her. Our curiosity is not satisfied over the exact reason for the purchase (were these

---

[2] Although she is unnamed in the Heb. (cf. NRSV: 'love a woman who has a lover and is an adulteress'), there need be no doubt that the woman in question is Hosea's wife (note the word *adulteress*, implying a married woman. Note too the charge to go to her *again*, and the parallel with Israel, the bride to whom God remains faithful). A variant reading of the expression *loved by* is possible, viz. 'in love with', as found in LXX (which also reads, less plausibly, 'evil', *ra'*, instead of *another man* or 'friend', *rēa'*). These alternatives involve only vowel changes, but there is no strong reason for preferring them to the standard text.

[3] David distributed them at the festivities to celebrate the ark's arrival at Jerusalem (2 Sam. 6:19). In a heathen context, Moab mourns the loss of them (Isa. 16:7). In the Song of Songs, the cry 'Strengthen me with raisins' (Song 2:5) is more accurately rendered 'with raisin cakes'.

[4] C. S. Lewis, *The Screwtape Letters* (Bles, 1942), IX.

her debts? was she now a slave? perhaps a prostitute working for an owner? or was this the compensation paid to the loving 'boyfriend' of verse 1 – revealing incidentally what his love was worth?). Nor are we told of Hosea's feelings: only how he scraped together the price he had to find.[5] In Scripture, more often than not, love is practical first, emotional only second; and it is always to be known by its fruits. This is not to say that love is 'as cold as charity', for the Old Testament largely uses, as we ourselves do, the same word for love between friends (e.g. 1 Sam. 18:3; 1 Kgs 5:1 [15, Heb.]) or between the sexes[6] as for the love that is the fulfilling of the law. The word takes its colour from its context (as its four occurrences in verse 1 have shown), but it is not complete without both aspects of self-giving: a devoted will and a genuine warmth.

There was realism as well as symbolism in the probationary period of verse 3. Its larger meaning is spelt out in verses 4–6, but within the marriage there were the disloyal habits of years to be broken, and the realities of personal relationship, which had hitherto stopped at the physical level, to be unhurriedly explored together. In the last part of verse 3 the NEB expresses the Hebrew text[7] as well as any: 'and have no intercourse with a man, nor I with you.'

Now follows the meaning of all this for Israel, the truant wife of Yahweh.

2. The hard way home (3:4–5)

Remember that a golden half-century was all that Hosea's hearers, for the most part, could recall, even though clouds were now forming in the distance. There was nothing but God's warning through Amos and Hosea to make disaster seem more than a remote possibility.

What is striking about this prophecy is first that it threatens the very pillars of life as Israel knew it, and then that it interprets the withdrawal of all these cherished things – good, bad and indifferent alike – as ultimate gain.

---

[5] It seems to have amounted to about 30 shekels, which is the price set on a slave in Exod. 21:32. See Wolff, p. 61, for this calculation. The load of barley was quite large, since a homer = 220 litres = c.6 bushels. If a lethek was half a homer, the total was about 330 litres, or 9 bushels.

[6] E.g. Gen. 29:18; Song 1:3, and the verbs throughout this book.

[7] The word 'another' in RSV is borrowed from LXX, whereas the Hebrew would include Hosea himself, who in the final clause is not merely promising to refrain from adultery but speaking of the postponement of marital intercourse.

These features of their life were certainly a mixture. At one extreme there was *sacrifice*, a major ordinance of God; at the other, *household gods* (or 'teraphim'; cf. Gen. 31:19), objects which violated the second commandment and were vigorously attacked by prophets and reformers from Samuel to Zechariah.[8] Between these extremes, *sacred stones*, or 'pillars', and *ephod* might be innocent or noxious in different situations,[9] while the existence of *king* and *prince* rather than some foreign governor and his regime had the welcome significance of a country at liberty.

But even the good or neutral things had been corrupted. Their kings and princes had been chosen in self-will ('without my consent', says God in 8:4) and in rejection of the house of David; and all their worship was tainted with Baalism. A clean break was needed, deep enough and long enough to make a new beginning possible: a pure return, in all humility, to the Lord himself; a renewal of the marriage that had seemed beyond repair.

An acid test of their sincerity comes in the words *and David their king*. In terms of the Israel which Hosea addressed, it meant a climbdown from their pride of independence from the southern tribes – from having their rival king, rival sanctuaries and priests and festivals, and their golden calves (1 Kgs 12:25–33). After the fall of their kingdom in 722 BC there was quite a trickle of such converts back to David's kingdom (see the comments on 1:10 – 2:1); but Hosea is looking far into the future to *the last days*.

We ourselves have seen the dawn of those days ('Dear children, this is the last hour', 1 John 2:18), and we, as believers, have inherited the name and destiny of Israel (see the final comments on chapter 2). If 'Israel' has taken on a richer meaning, so has *David their king*. Our Lord, in almost his last message to the church, takes up this royal name and proclaims himself not only David's offspring but also David's origin (Rev. 22:16). So our final verse captures the profound simplicity of the gospel. With the elaborate and humanly corrupted structures of verse 4 swept away, it portrays a people turning, seeking and coming to the Lord and his anointed, with deep penitence,[10] yet – in that they are turning *to his blessings* – with trust in what the New Testament will call his grace.

---

[8] See, e.g., 1 Sam. 15:23 (where 'idolatry' is lit. 'teraphim'); 2 Kgs 23:24; Zech. 10:2 (translated 'idols').

[9] Contrast the memorial 'stone pillars' of, e.g., Exod. 24:4 with the 'sacred stones' or 'pillars' (NRSV) of Baal worship (Deut. 12:3) which probably represented the male deity. Contrast also the ephod as a priestly garment (e.g. Exod. 28:4) with its use as an object of worship (Judg. 8:27).

[10] The expression translated *come trembling to the LORD* could be expressed more literally as 'tremble their way to the Lord'.

It may seem too much to see yet another level of fulfilment in this verse. But if (as I take it) Paul predicts in Romans 11:12, 15, 25ff. a great turning of the literal Israel to the Lord at the climax of the gospel era, the present verse may well have added for him its weight of confirmation to the promises he quotes, especially since there are allusions to our chapters not only in Romans 9:25–26 but in 11:30–32, the verses which round off his prediction.

Even at this early stage in the unfolding of the prophecy we can echo the substance of Paul's ensuing doxology in the remaining verses of Romans 11 – 'O the depth of the riches of the wisdom and knowledge of God!' – and more particularly his comment on these riches in Romans 5:20: 'Where sin increased, grace increased all the more.' On such a note, of God's *blessings* or 'goodness' (3:5), the opening chapters reach their satisfying end.

Part 2: The parable spelt out
HOW CAN I GIVE YOU UP?
(Hosea 4 – 14)

In Part 1, with the story and lessons of this extraordinary marriage, the book has already produced in bud the substance of its message, now to be unfolded further in what follows, along with social and political themes not touched on yet. But, more significantly, it has begun to do what no other Old Testament book does quite so vividly: to speak of God and his people not primarily in terms of master and servant, or king and subjects (indispensable as these categories are), but as man and wife, with all that this implies of personal delight and potential hurt.

This approach is far from sentimental. It sharpens guilt immeasurably by making it the betrayal of love; it shows us the true motive of God's persistence, so easily thought to be mere doggedness; and it deepens our understanding of repentance and renewal – for sins against love damage the very roots of a relationship, and are not healed by brisk apologies and hasty resolutions.

So the rest of the book will be packed with detail, whereas the opening chapters have painted the scene with only the broadest brush. It will plead for deep repentance, and it will extend the theme of personal relationships by pursuing that of father and child, as strikingly as the opening oracles explored the man-and-wife analogy.

It will be urgent and rapid, darting from one startling metaphor to another, drawing its pungent comparisons from human occupations, from nature and from Israel's family history. But it will end with an eloquent description of a people who have at last found their way home to God; and its epilogue will urge the reader to take this chequered story well to heart. It is more than a glimpse into history: it reveals the ways of God and the paths of life and death.

Hosea 4:1–19

6. A people without understanding

Any complacency the happy ending of the first three chapters may have induced in readers (if they have begun to picture God as the ever-accommodating husband) is now abruptly shattered. We are suddenly in a court of law, and God is prosecuting. He has no lack of charges to bring.

1. All the sins in the book (4:1–3)

The indictment is all the more telling in that it starts with what God pre-eminently looks for. He is weighing Israel in the balance against *faithfulness, love* and *acknowledgment of God*, only to find her wanting at every point: utterly light on all the things that matter. These three expressions lead us in from the outskirts of goodness to its heart and centre, and at each point God finds in his people this fatal lack. *Faithfulness* (Heb. *'ĕmet*) is common honesty or reliability, the first ingredient that we require for any dealings, however distant or impersonal, with others. *Love* (Heb. *ḥesed*, an important word with Hosea)[1] throws another weight into the scales, for it is the love and loyalty expected of partners in covenant – and this partnership was meant to embrace both the Lord and all one's fellow Israelites. What should have been a home and family had turned into a den of lust and violence.

As for the third and chief requirement, *acknowledgment* [or 'knowledge'] *of God*, any claim to it was already denied by the absence of the first two qualities. But note how high this last demand is pitched: not for a bare

---

[1] It is the word usually translated 'lovingkindness' in AV, RV, but in more recent versions the emphasis is on the element of constancy. E.g. NRSV chiefly translates it as 'steadfast love' (cf. 2:19; 6:6; 10:12), though here it has 'loyalty', and at 6:4 and 12:6, 'love'.

minimum of godliness, a decent fear of the Lord, fundamental though this is, but for a developed and developing relationship – for God is known as he is walked with and as his interests are shared and served. ('"Your father . . . defended the cause of the poor and needy, and so all went well with him. *Is that not what it means to know me?"* declares the LORD', Jer. 22:15–16.) We shall meet this high demand of fellowship again in the famous summary of what God most desires of his people ('mercy, not sacrifice, and acknowledgment of God rather than burnt offerings', 6:6), and shall be reminded in 13:4–5 of the grace that makes it possible: 'You shall acknowledge no God but me . . . *I cared for you* in the wilderness, in the land of burning heat.' In this book we are never far away from the warmly personal marital and father–child relationships as we explore God's expectations of us and his attitudes towards us.

Now follows in verse 2 the ugly catalogue of sins, a dark shadow of the Ten Commandments. Each of these evils meets us here full-blown, for it is a time of decadence and they have flourished virtually unchecked.

Scripture in general has two things to say about such rampant wickedness. On the one hand, it may question the boundaries we draw between serious and light offences, and between actions and attitudes, seeing for example (to go through this list) an inconsiderate word as little better than a curse (Prov. 27:14), insincerity as nothing but a lie (John 8:55), hatred as murder (1 John 3:15), meanness as theft (Mal. 3:8ff.) and lustful imaginings as mental adultery (Matt. 5:28). From its embryonic to its adult form, so to speak, a sin may change its names and its ability to hurt, but not its nature. That is one emphasis. The other is the one implicit here: that there is such a thing as monstrous and scarlet sin; that it is the business of teachers and rulers to restrain it (as the rest of the chapter and of the book will emphasize); and that the 'moral filth' – to borrow a phrase from James 1:21 – can reach a point where it is beyond all remedy (see, e.g., Jer. 7:16; Rev. 18). In Hosea that point is very near, and judgment must fall; but the punishment may yet produce a change of heart – a hope that runs through the book from the early chapters on the healing of the marriage to the final prospect of a blissful reunion in chapter 14.

Meanwhile to us, with our modern interest in ecology born of our new ability to make a desert of the world, the ensuing picture of a poisoned environment in verse 3 is all too familiar. But there is no reason to take it as describing Hosea's contemporary scene (as do NIV, NRSV and JB), for the tenses are those that normally indicate the future. It is a preview of God's judgment on corporate sin, which 'when it is full-grown, gives birth to death' on a wider scale than had once seemed possible (Jas 1:15). The Bible stresses sometimes the direct action of God in such a judgment, but sometimes too the reaction of his natural world to humanity's unnatural handling of it. It is put vividly in Leviticus 18, where a catalogue of perversions culminates in the warning, 'the land . . . will vomit you out as it vomited out the nations that were before you' (Lev. 18:28). If this language leaves out many links in the chain of causation, it is not hard to supply a few of them once one recognizes violence, lust and perversion as symptoms of the state of mind which will stop at no restraints and will sacrifice a whole future to the cravings of the moment. Hosea speaks here even more immediately to us, who are approaching the terminal stage of this infection, than to his own generation.

2. The guiltiest party (4:4–6)

Whatever we make of verse 4 (which is not as simple as it may look in our versions),[2] verse 6 removes all doubt that God's chief target is – in modern terms – the clergy. We can use that rough equivalent because it is the priests in their neglected capacity as teachers, not as sacrificers, who are now under fire. The prophets are no better, but here they are not the main concern.

What is even more striking than the poor showing of these men is the glory of the task entrusted to them: no less than to be the nation's spiritual educators. Unlike most religions, where priests were the close guardians of the cultic mysteries while the people's part was more or less mechanical, the faith of the Old Testament was a revelation addressed to every mind and conscience, 'making wise the simple'. Already in this chapter we have come across this theme, noting its profundity. Now we see it as not only profound but crucial: a matter of life and death. So a spiritually sightless priest is a mortal danger to himself and a disaster to others – for Hosea spells out in detail what Christ would one day sum up unforgettably in his saying on the blind who lead the blind (Matt. 15:14). The metaphor of stumbling in verse 5 leads on inexorably to harsher terms: *destroyed,*

---

[2] NRSV in 4b, 'O priest' (with which most of the newer versions broadly concur) fits the context well, but assumes that the Masoretic Text has suffered slightly in transmission. The latter reads, as in AV, RV, 'for thy people are as they that strive with the/a priest' (cf. NIV).

rejected and *ignored*; words which embrace the whole familiar world of these defaulters – their motherland, their priesthood, their posterity.

There is wrath as well as logic here, for the stumbling itself was no accident. All is traced to the emphatic *you* and to an act of will, as the Hebrew of verse 6 expresses it: *Because* you *have rejected knowledge . . .* And all is clinched in turn by God's no less emphatic *I also*, which brings the Hebrew sentence to a close.

3. Like people, like priests (4:7–10)

While it may look at first sight as if the Lord is speaking of the nation, growing in sin as it grows in size, the *they* of verse 8 means certainly the priests; therefore these men are surely the subject of verse 7 as well: *The more priests there were, the more they sinned against me.* And we can recognize the picture. A protected and exclusive group will easily grow arrogant, and then cynical and shameless. Added to this was the tempting fact that the sin offerings, which were prime lambs or kids, were priestly perquisites: 'The priest who offers it shall eat it' (Lev. 6:26).

So the charge of verse 8, *They feed on the sins of my people,* may be quite literal. To a degenerate set of priests, the more sin the better: there would be all the more fresh meat. The fact that the sin offering was a thing 'most holy . . . given to you' (as Moses reminded Aaron in Lev. 10:17) 'to take away the guilt of the community by making atonement for them' would mean nothing to them. On the other hand, since in times of moral decadence consciences grow hard, and sacrifices scarce, the meaning may be metaphorical: simply that the priests love and relish the prevailing wickedness.[3]

So comes the blunt prediction, *like people, like priests* – a saying which, taken on its own, might either brand the priests as, so to speak, clerical chameleons, forever matching their colour to their social context (a phenomenon by no means obsolete), or else, as the Hebrew idiom would equally allow, it might imply the converse: that the people would be sinking to the level of their priests.[4] But in fact it is a saying about

---

[3] As a point of detail not affecting the above alternatives, the Heb. words rendered here *They . . . relish* (8) are generally translated elsewhere by some such expression as 'to set one's heart on' something. Cf. NRSV/ RSV Deut. 24:15; Prov. 19:18. There is an instructive pair of occurrences in Pss. 24:4 and 25:1 (NIV '[put my] trust'; NRSV 'lift up their/my soul').

[4] The Heb. expression views the likeness as so complete that the parties compared can appear in either order. In, e.g., Gen. 18:25 the order is the opposite to the one we would employ ('as the righteous, so the wicked'), but elsewhere it may coincide with our use: e.g. Num. 15:15, 'as you are, so shall the sojourner be' (RSV).

judgment: a warning that there will be no exemptions. No privilege will shelter this supposed elite. There is a strikingly similar prophecy in Isaiah 24:1–3, speaking of the end time, where the same Hebrew phrase, 'like people, like priests', heads a list ('for priest as for people, for the master as for his servant', and so on) which demonstrates the equal exposure of us all to the day of God.

The terms of the coming judgment, as initially announced in verse 10, are distinctly appropriate. Food and sex have been these priests' obsession: food and sex will fail them, the one by shortage, the other by sterility – for it is a theme of Scripture and a fact of life that things material are precarious, and things merely sensual frustrating. Our Lord captured both these limitations in a single aphorism: 'Everyone who drinks this water will be thirsty again' (John 4:13). Of course, to *engage in prostitution* is a metaphor here for flirting with false gods; but it had a special aptness in view of the ritual fornication that was part of the attraction of these rivals, as verse 14b reminds us.

So, in what follows, the sins of the flesh and of the spirit intermingle. 'The fear of the Lord is clean' (Ps. 19:9, RSV); but even the noblest of other religions and philosophies can do little to cleanse the thoughts of human beings; and Canaanite religion perhaps least of all.

4. Creeping corruption (4:11–14)

In the Hebrew Bible the first word of this passage is *prostitution*, coming before *old wine and new wine* at the start of verse 11 (cf. RSV: 'Whoredom and wine and new wine take away the heart');[5] and the theme of unchastity, both figurative and literal, will dominate the paragraph. This opening thrust has the sound of a proverb, and Hosea will clinch the message with another at the end of verse 14. Both of these sayings chime in with the charge against the priests that they had left their people at the mercy of any folly that took their fancy – 'destroyed' (as verse 6 has put it) 'from lack of knowledge'.

---

[5] It is transposed to the end of verse 10 in the layout of *BH* and *BHS* and of most modern versions to provide an object to 'give themselves to' at the end of that verse. It may have originally come twice, ending verse 10 and opening 11, and have dropped out once in the copying (such 'haplography' is a common slip of the pen); or else verse 10 should perhaps be translated, with AV/RV, '. . . left off to take heed to the Lord'. The prominence of 'prostitution' in 11–14 supports the inclusion of the word here, in agreement with the Masoretic punctuation.

In itself, the proverb about prostitution and wine makes the point that what unbridled drinking does to blur the mind, unbridled sex will also do in its more subtle way. This is a remark well suited to a pleasure-loving Israel; but Hosea makes the further point that spiritual wantonness, the deserting of God for idols, is equally bemusing. The very fact that a people once enlightened by the living God could turn to bits of wood for guidance – praying to a wooden idol and, for divination, studying the way a stick thrown up at random might fall and point (cf. Ezek. 21:21) – told its tale of spiritually clouded minds. Such things were for 'the heathen in his blindness'. 'The nations', Moses had said of the Canaanites,

> listen to those who practise sorcery or divination. But as for you, the LORD your God has not permitted you to do so. The LORD your God will raise up for you a prophet like me from among you, from your fellow Israelites. You must listen to him.
> (Deut. 18:14–15)

As for idols, the heathen themselves should have known better than to worship them, but their minds were darkened and in bondage (Isa. 44:18–20).

Whatever excuse there might be for these other nations, for Israel there was none. Their infatuation was deliberate, a surrender to *a spirit of prostitution* that had all the excitement of an elopement or an orgy. This, they felt, was freedom! Instead of high demands on mind and will there were the myths and magic of the corn god. Instead of the remoteness of the temple, so unfairly situated in the rival capital, Jerusalem, there was the appeal of hilltop sanctuaries to local pride and superstition, and the attractiveness of tree-shrines *where* (as God observes with fine scorn) *the shade is pleasant*! Hosea's runaway wife had felt the lure of just such trivialities in her escape from home and husband.

But the language of adultery and prostitution was not all metaphor. This society had gone as sex-mad as our own, with promiscuous adolescents and with marriages violated from the start. Hosea takes an unexpected line on this, for instead of castigating the juvenile prostitutes (*your daughters*) and the roving brides, he asks who has set them this example. The answer is the men – the very fathers and husbands who felt themselves betrayed.

Verse 14 is in fact a landmark in moral history by its refusal to treat a man's sexual sins more leniently than a woman's. That double standard had been brutally taken for granted, long before, by Jacob's fourth son, Judah, who thought nothing of visiting a prostitute but reacted to his daughter-in-law's apparent unchastity with 'Bring her out and let her be burned to death!' (Gen. 38:24).

The whole paragraph in fact insists on joining together what we might wish to treat as separate issues. It looked first at self-indulgent, mindless religion; found it guilty of producing spiritual adultery ('they have deserted the LORD to give themselves to prostitution', 10–11); saw this in turn as the direct cause of moral breakdown (note the *Therefore* of verse 13c); brought to light men's heavy share in women's guilt; and in the same breath swept aside the accepted difference between going with harlots and going with cult-prostitutes. This last point throws a lurid light on Canaanite religion, which owed much of its appeal to the belief that one's crops could be magically made fertile through a sacrifice and sex act at the sanctuary. The fact that our terms 'cult-prostitutes', 'temple prostitutes', and the like, translate a single word meaning literally 'holy women' shows the unbridgeable gulf between the values of the two religions. Biblical and pagan holiness do not inhabit the same world.

One might add that the modern paganism which sees profundity in the 'dark gods', and more sublimity in a *grande passion* than in a single stead-fast love, is as fatal a parody of the truth as was Baalism in its time. But today the concept in dispute is not holiness, which only one side talks about, but love.

The passage is capped in 14c by a tersely devastating saying – just four words in the Hebrew – which could well be coupled with the verse that introduced the paragraph, thus (freely):

(11) Wenching and wining addle the mind
(14c) And the folk who won't think won't survive.

No political initiatives, no social engineering, could save a people in this state of mindless apostasy. Nothing but repentance.

5. Keep your distance! (4:15–19)

Irony, bitter irony, is surely the clue to this sudden shout of warning to the neighbouring Judah. It is unimaginative to ask what such a change of audience is doing here,[6] or whether it is Israel or Judah who is being warned away from the places and practices of verse 15. As Mays points out, 'Whether Judeans were inclined to visit Gilgal and Bethel is beside the point. The exhortation to Judah not to visit Israel's favourite shrines is . . . meant for the ears of those who did worship in them.' It was a startling, infuriating thing for Israelites to hear – far more effective than a straight onslaught.

Hosea is in fact taking a leaf out of Amos's book. Amos, a lover of surprise, had ironically invited his readers to both these famous shrines, to deepen their guilt! 'Go to Bethel and sin . . .' (Amos 4:4). Join our pilgrimage and earn a black mark! Hosea's variation on the theme gets under the skin at two fresh points. It makes a wounding comparison, presenting Israel as no fit company for her smaller sister; and it invents a nickname for the royal shrine: no longer Bethel, 'house of God', but Beth Aven, 'house of evil' – for God cannot own such a place, or have his name bandied about by those who think of him as Baal. You cannot keep the third commandment, against taking his name in vain, while you blithely flout the first two.

If we want a modern equivalent, it could well be the religious pluralism expressed in the studied neutrality of certain courses on world religions, or of any multifaith service. 'Come to St X's and blaspheme,' a modern Amos might say. And a modern Hosea: 'Don't darken its doors! You must choose between that and God.'

What follows in the rest of this short passage brings to mind our Lord's lament, 'How often I have longed . . . and you were not willing' (Matt. 23:37). The question[7] *How then can* [or more accurately, 'Will'] *the* LORD . . . ? (16b) confronts us with the obstinate realities of the situation, and there will be still more searching questions later, notably in 6:4 and in God's anguished soliloquy of chapter 11. For the moment, in face of such stubbornness, nothing will win a right response. The prodigal must be left to his boon companions (this is the force of NIV's

---

[6] A common suggestion is that a later editor has sought to widen the relevance of the book by inserting this and other references to the sister kingdom of Judah. This is easy to assert, but the frequency of such passages (1:1, 7, 11; 4:15; 5:5, 10, 12–14; 6:4, 11; 8:14; 10:11; 11:12; 12:2), the breadth of vision of other prophets (e.g. Amos of Judah prophesied to Israel) and the similar temptations that beset both kingdoms tell against the assumption that Hosea would have had no thoughts for the southerners.

[7] Literally it has the form of a statement, but spoken with an irony that dismisses it, as the context demands. Cf., e.g., Gen. 3:1, 'Did God really say . . . ?'; or Gen. 18:12, 'Sarah laughed to herself as she thought, "After I am worn out . . . will I now have this pleasure?"' – interpreted in the next verse as meaning, 'Will I really . . . ?'

word *joined*, 17) and to his revels and their aftermath. Not till then (and here not till the last line of the chapter) is there any prospect of his coming to himself.

Hosea 5:1–14

7. The prospect darkens

For several chapters now the picture will be building up by fragments, coming at the subject from all kinds of angles. By its very disjointedness the style suits the chaotic situation it addresses. Here and there in this chapter some belated stirrings of national alarm will be detected; but what action it will lead to is quite another matter. How deep or shallow the change of mood is will be the question particularly faced in chapter 6. Meanwhile God's exposure of his people and of what must happen to them continues in a hail of strong and lively metaphors.

1. A nation to avoid (5:1–2)

So far, the brunt of the attack has been on the priests (4:4ff.). Now God rounds on those who have so willingly been led by them. The royal court will have its special reprimand in 7:1–7, but for the present all three estates of the realm are equally under fire.[1]

God sees them as a menace – this people called to be a blessing to the world! The label once fastened on the Canaanites, and also proverbially on prostitutes, comparing them to snares and traps, must now be pinned upon the chosen people. The place names of verse 1 were famous in their history: Mizpah was associated perhaps with Jacob, perhaps with Jephthah, Samuel and Saul (for there were several places bearing this name, 'the watchtower'), and Tabor with the great victory of Deborah and

---

[1] Possibly, however, since *judgment* can mean 'justice', the fourth line of verse 1 intensifies the guilt of those in authority by saying that justice is their (neglected) responsibility (cf. JB). Yet such a meaning, if intended, could have been expressed more plainly.

Barak. Now they were infamous. To get caught up with what was done there was to wander into a trap, like some hapless bird or beast.

Hosea's audience would need no telling why he was attacking these places; and even we, without their local knowledge, have the clue we need in 4:13. If many an ordinary hilltop had its Baal shrine, wooing dozens of frequenters away from the true faith, the shrines on high places as famous as Mizpah and Mount Tabor would seduce their hundreds.[2]

Modern prophets would scandalize even the faithful if they started naming the equivalents of apostate Mizpah and Tabor. Among the theological faculties where would they begin? Where would they end? Which of these poses no threat to the faith of its initiates? And among the vocational colleges and seminaries, the societies, movements and churches? As the reader will observe, the present author lacks the courage of Hosea; but, more to the point, he lacks Hosea's infallibility! The application of the prophet's words is better done by self-examination; but it should indeed be done.

2. No short way home (5:3–7)

We can be grateful to the NEB for the affectionate tone it gives to the opening words, translating them as

> I have cared for Ephraim
> and I have not neglected Israel;
> but now . . .

– for even though this may press the declaration 'I *know* all about Ephraim' rather far, it rightly draws attention to Ephraim's unresponsiveness (4b, *they do not acknowledge/*'care nothing for'), and it makes the valid point that God's knowing is never perfunctory or cold. To Hosea, of all the prophets, this was crucial; and elsewhere in the Old Testament the deep thrust of God's knowledge, however painful it may initially be, is seen as something to be welcomed, for it means that he knows the worst, and yet persists with us. 'I have seen their ways, but I will heal them' (Isa. 57:18).

---

[2] 'A pit . . . in Shittim' (NRSV; cf. GNB) slightly emends a difficult Heb. text. It provides a third place name and variety of trap, but remains a conjecture. The existing text appears to mean 'and devious men [or apostates] have deepened slaughter' (cf. NIV). 'Deepened' is interpreted by JB as 'are entrenched in', and by NEB as 'have shown base (ingratitude)'. G. R. Driver (*JTS* 34 [1933], p. 40) argues for the meaning 'they deepened the corruption (i.e. fornication) of Shittim' – a reference to the notorious incident of Num. 25:1ff.

But there is no pretence here that reconciliation can be easy, or penitence a mere gesture of apology. The whole book is, from one angle, a study of what it means to turn back to God. So in this passage the nation is confronted with two unconsidered facts: the stranglehold of its own habits, and the hiddenness of God for worshippers who are insincere.

The first of these is swiftly demonstrated, point after point, in verses 4 and 5. To say that *Their deeds do not permit them to return* may well have a double meaning: not only that sinners are the prisoners of their habits, but that their actions, persisted in, will unsay their pious words. The second half of the verse delves deeper, beneath the habits to the fickle spirit, and beneath the fickleness itself to the fundamental lack: *they do not acknowledge the LORD*. This is the hiatus at the heart of all nominal religion. But verse 5 points out another obstacle to a reunion. Sin not only alienates: it saddles one with guilt – and guilt is written all over this nation, not by the shamefaced looks that normally betray it, but by the very brazenness that would deny it.

So they must learn that God is not the prisoner of his sacraments. Verse 6 sees them going through the due procedures of religion, sparing no expense to gain access to God; but there is nobody at home. It is a spectacle that meets us in all the prophets of the time; for this was a religious age, and if there is one thing more odious to God than plain iniquity it is what Isaiah 1:13 calls 'worthless assemblies' – surpliced sin, aggravated in this case by the fertility rites which produced a crop of *illegitimate children* in both senses of the word, literal and spiritual. All this may explain the cryptic mention of the disastrous 'new moon'[3] in verse 7, for (as Isaiah went on to say) 'Your New Moon feasts and your appointed festivals I hate with all my being' (Isa. 1:14). The very festivals that were relied on to placate God would be the sharpest provocation of him.

Yet his anger is that of love, not hate. His relentless harrying of them is designed to bring them home, as passage after passage will make plain.

---

[3] This could mean 'a month will (suffice to) devour them' (cf. AV). Dividing the words differently and revocalizing them, NEB reads 'an innovator', which it interprets as 'an invader'. Other suggestions ('destroyer', 'locust', etc.) assume a miscopying of consonants (cf. LXX, but not the other Greek versions). The standard text, however, as in RV, NRSV, is intelligible and pungent. See NIV margin.

3. Deep trouble (5:8–14)

The first part of the chapter brought us up short with its double rebuff to Israel. God was withdrawing, we were told (6), and judgment was imminent (7). Now we pick up the second of these threads, leaving the threat of withdrawal to reappear in the next section, where it will introduce one of the book's most notable chapters.

For the present, then, the theme is national disaster. It was no empty threat: the northern kingdom (called both 'Israel' and 'Ephraim' in these chapters) was wiped out in 722 BC, and the southern kingdom, Judah and Benjamin, was brought to its knees in 701, surviving by a hair's breadth, only to collapse little more than a century later.

The place names that open this oracle (8) straddle the border of the two kingdoms – a warning that the invader would penetrate Israel right to its southernmost extremity, to the alarm of the Benjaminite Gibeah and Ramah, which lay only just beyond that boundary, even as the doomed Beth Aven (i.e. Bethel; see on 4:15) lay just within it.

They might well tremble. If Israel was a den of vice, Judah was a den of thieves – for the habit of land-grabbing in verse 10[4] is witnessed by the contemporary Micah and Isaiah:

They covet fields and seize them,
  and houses, and take them.
They defraud people of their homes,
  they rob them of their inheritance.
(Mic. 2:2)

Shame on you! you who add house
  to house and join field to field,
  until not an acre remains,
and you are left to dwell alone in the land.
(Isa. 5:8, NEB)

The opening alarm calls presage war; but the human invader is so clearly a mere tool of judgment that he goes unmentioned here. God's

---

[4] This may, however, be an analogy for the removal of moral landmarks. The expression *like those*... may indicate either this analogy or a comparison of these expropriating creditors and officials with the criminals who surreptitiously moved boundary stones, attracting the curse of Deut. 27:17.

anger and God's action are everything, and the different roles in which he now appears are startling and instructive. When he likens himself to a panther (14, NEB) or a lion (NIV), it is no stylized picture but a lifelike predator, grimly purposeful and dangerous. But verse 12 presents a quite novel impression of God in action: *like a moth*[5] . . . *like rot* (or caries?) – for the silent process of decay is his, no less than the march of armies. Both can be well accounted for in natural terms when a nation goes soft, but both are God's potential scourges, as appropriate as they are deadly. Of the two threats to a people, aggression and corruption, the second is the more ominous, and in these chapters its signs are everywhere. Aggression, for all its terrors, can unite and purge, but corruption only divides and demoralizes.

But when this nation does wake up to its predicament, according to this chapter its reaction is typically shallow. To save its skin – never mind its soul! – it flies straight to Assyria,[6] asking itself no questions about the kind of patron it is getting, still less about the kind of cure it really needs.

What makes the deal look even less promising is the probability that Hosea is speaking of the desperate payment scraped together for Assyria by Israel's King Menahem. This was meant not only to buy off an invasion already begun, but to get external backing for Menahem's precarious kingship – for he was a usurper who had waded through particularly vile slaughter to the throne. His story, which included the butchery of a whole town's pregnant women, is summarized in 2 Kings 15:16–22.

To us, who know the eventual outcome, there is heavy irony in this diplomatic stroke. Menahem's regime was duly propped up, but within twenty years Assyria proved to be the very nation marked out as Israel's executioner.

With some premonition of this, Israel would soon start flitting from one great power to another, playing off Egypt against Assyria, and Assyria against Egypt. The later chapters will have many remarks about it. But first there is a glimmer of light, for which our present chapter's final verse will set the scene.

---

[5] Or possibly 'like putrefaction' (K-B), a conjecture by G. R. Driver from an Arabic root. Although this is precarious it gains some probability from verse 13's allusion to an unhealed wound.

[6] *The great king* (13) makes an appropriate parallel to *Assyria*, whose kings used such a title. The Heb. text allows this if its consonants are redivided and revocalized; and this seems a reasonable reconstruction. As it stands, however, it reads 'king Jareb' (AV, RV), i.e. 'a king who finds fault', 'a king who will contend' (NRSV mg.), or 'King Pick-Quarrel' (G. A. Smith) – a fitting enough label for Tiglath-pileser III and his successors.

Hosea 5:15 – 7:2

8. Let us press on to know the LORD

Here we reach a high point among the foothills of the prophecy, from which we catch a tantalizing glimpse of the distant summit, the final chapter. Even though we plunge almost immediately into as dark a valley as any that we encounter, we have first had an unforgettable if only momentary view of a goal worth reaching at any cost.

1. The reunion God longs for (5:15 – 6:6)

There was a warning earlier on (5:6) that Israel would one day seek the Lord but find no trace of him:

> they will not find him;
>> he has withdrawn himself from them.

Now we look at both sides of this. First the withdrawal. From one angle, this is only what the fickle wife deserves, so long as she plays fast and loose with her true partner; and God has already spoken in terms of such deserving. Yet even the outburst of chapter 2, which threatened famine and disgrace as her due punishment (2:13, summing up a catalogue of ordeals), had melted into the language of appeal and courtship:

> Therefore I am now going to allure her;
>> I will lead her into the wilderness
>> and speak tenderly to her.
> (2:14)

Throughout the book this is the longed-for outcome of his judgments. Whatever else might be their character, they are pre-eminently a lover's short-lived coolness to reawaken love.

But what are we to make of Israel's response?

As God describes it (5:15) and quotes it (6:1–3), it is a model of repentance, entreaty and trust. Yet he seems to greet it with profound misgiving in verses 4ff.

There are at least two ways of taking this. One is that God is first portraying in 5:15 – 6:3 the deep conversion that he is working for and will at last evoke – that total change of heart which will irradiate the closing chapter of the book. Then in verses 4ff. he turns to the sad spectacle of Israel as she is at present, incapable of any such response. On this view (or on the view that verses 1–3 are Hosea's own plea to Israel – see below) no fault can be found with the sentiments of these verses. In themselves they are a perfect expression of humility, faith and serious intent. The trouble is that Israel is at present in no state to speak or even think along such lines. Religion, for her, is not *knowing* God, still less 'pressing on to know him' (cf. NRSV). It is merely placating him with sacrifice, as verse 6 implies.

A more common view[1] is that the fine words of verses 1–3 are Israel's own, but facile and presumptuous, as if to say with German poet Heinrich Heine, '*Dieu me pardonnera, c'est son métier*' – 'God will forgive me, that's his trade' – making light of both the desperate state of the nation (*After two days he will revive us*) and the high demands of pressing on to know the Lord. Against this one might point out that this speech is introduced in 5:15 as something spoken out of deep distress, and that the second word for *seek* in that verse is especially urgent (*earnestly seek*: cf. NEB, NIV). Yet a similar passage in the Psalms reveals how false such earnestness can be:

> Whenever God slew them, they would seek him;
>> they eagerly turned to him again . . .
> But then they would flatter him with their mouths,
>> lying to him with their tongues;
> their hearts were not loyal to him.
> (Ps. 78:34, 36–37)

---

[1] Cf. the headings in JB, GNB, and the light-hearted tone adopted in the latter's rendering of 6:1–3.

Either view, then, is possible, and either way it emerges that Israel has no conception of the faithful love that God is looking for. But to me it is the former view that carries conviction, if only because the divine protest in verse 6 makes no contact – except by way of agreement! – with anything in verses 1–3. It also allows us to read these verses as the eloquent and rich example of a serious approach to God which they appear to be. They are restored to us as words not only for study but for actual use.

To look at the passage, then, more closely, it is significant that the word 'saying' or 'beg my favour' at the end of 5:15 in RSV and NRSV (cf. GNB) is no part of the Hebrew text, but is borrowed from the Septuagint. Without it, we are free to read 6:1–3 either as the expected words of Israel or as Hosea's own call to his compatriots: an inspired appeal for which, however, Israel is not yet remotely ready (as verses 4ff. make clear), although one day she will be (as chapter 14 foresees).

There are several further points to notice in this great passage (as I regard it), above and beyond those that lie so richly on the surface. One of these is the word *return*, which plays a major part in the book – naturally enough in view of the theme of God's reclaiming of his bride, first acted out in miniature in Hosea's home. Since it means not only 'return' but more basically 'turn', it can be the very picture either of desertion and estrangement, as one party turns his or her back upon the other,[2] or, more happily, of renouncing such a course and turning to be reunited. So, in this better sense, it embraces both repentance and conversion, crowned with reconciliation. The word is as strong as it is simple.

Among other points in verses 1–3 we can note how *He has torn* (1) picks up the violent word of 5:14 ('tear', or 'maul', NEB) and how it sees, behind the trauma of invasion, not just the savagery of humanity but the judgment and discipline of God. The classic model of this constructive attitude to calamity, deserved or undeserved, is in Joseph's words, 'You intended to harm me, but God intended it for good' (Gen. 50:20).

Notice, again, how radical a cure is looked for. Bandaging and healing (1) provide one way of expressing it, but bringing back to life (2) does better justice to humanity's plight and to God's power. Admittedly the words *revive* and *restore* need mean no more than 'heal' and 'recover'; but they

---

[2] The noun from this verb is rendered at 11:7 'turn from' (NIV), 'turning away' (NRSV), 'rebellion' (NEB), etc., and at 14:4 (5, Heb.) 'waywardness' (NIV), 'disloyalty' (NRSV), 'faithlessness' (RSV) or, better, 'apostasy' (NEB). With a very different motive God has just spoken in 5:15 of his turning and going away, to bring Israel to her senses.

can also and more properly express the meeting of a need as desperate as that which faced Ezekiel in the vision of his people as a heap of dry bones, or Paul in his diagnosis of humanity as 'dead in . . . transgressions and sins' (Ezek. 37:1–14; Eph. 2:1). Nothing short of resurrection is fit to describe such need and such salvation; and while the mention of *the third day* would sound to Hosea's hearers as the mere equivalent of 'very soon', the prophet may have spoken more significantly than he knew (cf. 1 Pet. 1:10–12); for it is only in Christ's resurrection that his people are effectively raised up, as both Paul and Peter teach us (1 Cor. 15:17; Eph. 2:5–6; 1 Pet. 1:3). And when Paul finds, apparently, not only the resurrection but even 'the third day' to be 'according to the Scriptures' (1 Cor. 15:4), it is at least possible – though one should put it no higher – that this passage as well as 'the sign of Jonah' was in his mind.

Then the call 'Let us know, let us press on to know the LORD' (3, NRSV) lifts the appeal decisively above the plane of mere national survival to that of a growing relationship with God.[3] This anticipates not only the climax of the great verse 6, 'the knowledge of God' (NRSV), but also our Lord's own definition of the content of eternal life, as to 'know you, the only true God, and Jesus Christ, whom you have sent' (John 17:3). It is, after all, a *marriage* that God is concerned with; nothing less. So the perseverance which the first line of the verse invites is more than matched from God's side, using the lovely metaphors of the unfailing sunrise[4] and the transforming rains.

After all this, the anticlimax of verse 4 is shattering – as heartbreaking, we may feel, as our own performance:

'Your love is like the morning mist,
    like the early dew that disappears.'

Heartbreaking indeed; but met with neither a helpless wringing of hands nor a pointless flash of temper. The fierceness of verse 5, with its cutting in pieces and killing, is not blind fury, but has the clarity of light, the purity of justice[5] and the constructiveness of love – for verse 6 reveals the end in

---

[3] Cf. Paul's ambition 'to know Christ', as he 'presses on' (Phil. 3:10–16).

[4] The RSV's translation 'going forth' suits not only the idea of a person's setting out on a journey or an errand, but of the sun's majestic emergence to run its course: cf. Ps. 19:6 (7, Heb.).

[5] Verse 5c is a half-line, hence NEB transfers it to precede verse 3's half-line (*he will appear* etc.). But it has an important function in verse 5, whether as read in NIV (*my judgments*, as in LXX, Syr.) or as in NRSV mg. ('your judgement', i.e. 'your justice', as in MT, anticipating Israel's chastened return to moral integrity).

view. Notice, too, the implied appeal to reason and conscience, for the 'cutting and killing' was done by *my prophets* first of all. God does not send his judgments without warning or without the offer of repentance.

Verse 6 was a saying highly treasured by our Lord: see Matthew 9:13; 12:7. Like the two great commandments which he picked out as the ruling principles of the law, it pinpoints the supportive relationship to our fellows and the filial relationship to God that are the heart of true religion. It is a theme of all Hosea's great contemporaries, stirring them to some of their most powerful pronouncements: for example, Isaiah 1:12–17; Amos 5:21–24; Micah 6:6–8.

2. The rebuff to God's advances (6:7 – 7:2)

For all Hosea's highlighting of Israel's broken marriage and God's tenacious love, his prophecy is always well 'earthed', quick to expose the unromantic social cost of Israel's marital adventures. Here as ever the tragic and the squalid intertwine. Spiritually, there is the tragedy of her cast-off marriage vows (6:7) and of her *prostitution* (10) in taking up with any customer – any pagan deity or cultic novelty – that comes along. Morally and socially, we see the squalor of a lawless society, with not only thieves and bandits spreading terror (7:1) but the very priests turning religion into a heartless, even murderous racket.[6] (Jesus was to find the same. Perhaps the church today can be grateful to be without the power that offers this temptation!)

The place names in this passage would obviously waken embarrassing memories for Hosea's hearers, though we no longer have the clues to them. This hardly matters: in fact it emphasizes his concern – which is also God's – with what is very local, very topical, as well as with the wider sweep of history. As J. L. Mays has strikingly observed, '6:7–10 is a sort of miniature guidebook to the geography of sin in Israel; going from one place to another it catalogues the famous crimes of various localities as an indictment of the whole nation.'

In NIV and most modern versions, *Adam* is treated as the name of one of these towns, and the reading 'Like Adam' (6:7, 'Like Adam, they have

---

[6] The talk of *murder on the road to Shechem* (6:9) may be a strong way of saying that the pilgrims lured to this paganized sanctuary go there to their spiritual destruction (see on 4:15). Or it may be literal, referring to some recent outrage or to a continuing vendetta. H. W. Wolff suggests, e.g., that Shechem, far from being paganized, may have been too orthodox for the liking of its rival shrines, so that its pilgrims went in danger of their lives. We simply do not know enough.

broken the covenant') is taken to be an error for *As at Adam* . . . There is no textual basis for this change, which seems to rob the verse of a powerful comparison (as, incidentally, they rob Job 31:33 of the same phrase for no good reason), but it must be admitted that the next line, 'they were unfaithful to me *there*', is hard to account for if no place has yet been mentioned.[7]

The final verse in this section, as we have divided it at 7:2, is the most alarming of all, and it breathes a very modern atmosphere. People's bland dismissal of any question of divine judgment has made repentance virtually unthinkable. One is reminded of the veiled amusement with which (at the time of writing these comments) a leading broadcaster reported a local church's arrangement of a day of prayer for national repentance during a time of exceptional industrial bitterness. To him and, by implication, to the bulk of his hearers, God was laughably irrelevant. To God, by contrast, a people and its sins are anything but irrelevant. To paraphrase this verse, guilt does not fade with time; it wraps a people round; it stares God in the face.

---

[7] A possible answer is that Hosea is speaking of a realm of behaviour, not a locality. Cf. G. A. F. Knight (Torch Commentary, 1960): 'THERE, in this very matter of keeping covenant . . .' Those, however, who argue for a locality point out (a) that Josh. 3:16 mentions a place named Adam, and (b) that the Heb. prefix *b* ('at') is easily confused with *k* ('like'), although the ancient versions agree with the Heb. text here against the modern emendation.

Hosea 7:3–16

9. Decadence

Some of Hosea's most brilliant similes are clustered here, as he exposes the corruption of the palace, the nation, the diplomats and even the prayers that people utter. But he is not scoring points. God's concern is that of a father for a son who refuses to be helped. This revealing relationship, mentioned in passing in verse 15, will be taken up again and sensitively explored in chapter 11.

1. Corruption at court (7:3–7)

This lurid scene is the culmination of the previous section, which brought us from the country towns to Samaria, the capital. Now we penetrate the palace, to find the king and his courtiers not only doing nothing to stem the tide of evil, but revelling in it, titillated by it, relishing the prevailing graft and trickery (3), and letting their lusts take over. The picture of the oven that needs no stoking once the fermentation has begun tells its own story of self-propagating passion – but Hosea will give a further twist to this simile before he finishes.

The royal anniversary (5) should have had the stamp of greatness on it, rising to the vision of such a psalm as 72:

> Endow the king with your justice, O God,
>   the royal son with your righteousness . . .
> May he be like rain falling on a mown field,
>   like showers watering the earth.

> In his days may the righteous flourish,
>> and prosperity abound till the moon is no more.
> (Ps. 72:1, 6–7)

Instead, it was an orgy. In a few biting phrases Hosea evokes the scene for us, with its sprawling, flushed and ribald fools: a scene repeated often enough where boasters (from Ben-Hadad and his allies 'getting drunk' before a battle [1 Kgs 20:16], to the doomed Belshazzar, drinking toasts to his gods from the temple vessels [Dan. 5]) and escapists like these 'vain and light persons' try to transcend themselves with the help of what they swallow. Amos at about this time was encountering the same flight from reality, conducted admittedly with more finesse, among the dilettanti of Israel and Judah; but Isaiah paints an even more revolting picture than Hosea's of the kind of party that we find here – and in his oracle the chief revellers are, of all people, priests and prophets (see Amos 6:1–7; Isa. 28:7ff.).

Now (reverting to Hosea's simile) the banked-up fire of verse 4, that pleasurable build-up of shared lust, bursts into a frightening blaze, as passions flare not merely into lechery (as in verse 4) but into murder (6–7) – for when passion reigns there are no limits or loyalties. With such a fever running at every level of society, it was no coincidence that Israel's last three decades were a turmoil of intrigue, as one conspirator after another hacked his way to the throne, only to be murdered in his turn. Of the six men who reigned in those thirty years, four were assassins, and only one died in his own bed.[1]

2. A nation of unteachables (7:8–16)

It is one scathing picture after another: the inedible cake, the first grey hairs, the flustered bird, the flawed weapon. Poor Israel! Poor church, perhaps?

It may be gilding the lily to add anything to these vignettes, but each of them has more content than a first glance may take in.

On the first of them (8) George Adam Smith has been quoted again and again, but his comment deserves it: 'How better describe a half-fed people,

---

[1] The last king, Hoshea, may have escaped a violent end, but he died in captivity. The four assassinations are recorded in 2 Kgs 15:10, 14, 25, 30.

a half-cultured society, a half-lived religion, a half-hearted policy, than by a half-baked scone?'[2] The first line of this couplet, *Ephraim mixes with the nations*, brings out the loss of conviction which left this people neither one thing nor the other: neither a light to the Gentiles nor an excusable product of paganism. The church in every age knows this temptation, and tends to meet it either by retreat into itself or by melting into its surroundings. The Gospels demonstrate a better way in their account of the good physician and the friend of sinners: wholly himself yet wholly accessible, and as compassionate as he was uncompromising.

The second figure, of the man who thinks himself still in his prime (9), may recall to us (in muted terms) the plight of Samson, his strength devoured by the aliens whom he loved and hated, while 'he did not know that the Lord had left him' (Judg. 16:20). For Israel there has been as yet no rude awakening like his. To this people, if not to others, the decline is doubly imperceptible, unnoticed through its gradualness and invisible to their pride. Yet the arrogance itself is a telltale sign of it – almost like the hardening lines in a face[3] – and a fatal obstacle to their even considering repentance. We noticed at 5:4–5 the inhibiting influence of the sinner's cherished ways and attitudes. The repetition here of 5:5a (*Israel's arrogance testifies against him*) draws attention to the most damning and also most addictive of sin's ingredients. The victim, as our verse 10 sadly observes, would rather not be helped.

The third simile, the frantic dove (11–12), lends a cartoonist's wit and verve to a theme already touched on at 5:13, one which will reappear at intervals from now on. To put it prosaically, the theme is Israel's diplomatic duplicity, for she kept faith with no-one, least of all with God, but changed alliances with every shift of the political wind. We saw how King Menahem bought Assyria's patronage (2 Kgs 15:19).[4] His son's assassin, Pekah, went back on this alignment as soon as it ceased to suit him – and lost half his kingdom (2 Kgs 15:29).[5] His successor, Hoshea, followed his example and lost the rest – for after renewing the allegiance he broke it by intrigue with Egypt, only to lose what little remained of his realm for ever (2 Kgs 17:1–6).

---

[2] Smith, p. 273. The flat loaf or cake in question would be of dough baked either on hot stones or pressed against the side of an oven. Not turned over, one side would be burnt, the other uncooked. Was this a memory from the stormy marriage?

[3] One could even translate 10a 'Israel's pride shows [lit. 'answers', as in a mirror] in his face'.

[4] See above, p. 50.

[5] In 2 Kgs 16:5ff. and Isa. 7:1ff. we read of Pekah's alliance with Syria (Aram) and his attempt to force Judah into an anti-Assyrian league.

All this was *senseless*; but it was worse: it was desertion and rebellion – and not only politically but, as God says in verse 13, 'from *me*', 'against *me*'. This is the dimension the opportunist always forgets. So the darting diplomats, flitting from patron to patron like birds from tree to tree, were to fly straight into the one peril they had overlooked: the net of divine judgment. Yet characteristically Hosea gives us not only the sentence that must be passed on them, but God's rueful comment on it:

> *I long to redeem them,*
>> *but they speak about me falsely.*

For what can even God do for the insincere? We get a glimpse in verse 14 of their kind of praying ('Never mind about "Your kingdom come" – where's our daily bread?'). It was all self-pity and piling on the pressure by self-mutilation, more like the blackmail of a child's tantrum than a genuine heart-cry. That was how one prayed to Baal,[6] not to the Lord; and whether or not the actual name of Baal should occur in verse 16,[7] God reads it at least between the lines, and is as hurt as he is angry. To rebel (14c) is bad enough, but what the Lord repeatedly points out through Hosea (a prophet sensitized to this through his own unhappy past) is that they are sinning against love. It was a husband's love in chapter 2; but now, and supremely in chapter 11, it is a father's, with a glimpse in verse 15a of that tenderness, care and pride with which this father has sought to make a man of his son Israel.

The chapter ends bleakly. Its threat of *sword* and *ridicule* is not arbitrary. To betray and belittle everything to which one owes most (notice *their insolent words*, 16) is a sure mark of decadence; and decadence is an invitation to the predator. It is also cynicism, and the cynical get the friends they deserve, who are sure to find their plight merely amusing (16b).

We are left, too, with the fourth of this chapter's scathing pictures: the flawed weapon of verse 16a. (For the others, see the first remarks on this

---

[6] Cf. 1 Kgs 18:28, if *slash*, rather than 'gather', is the right reading in our verse 14, as LXX and some Heb. MSS suggest (see NIV mg.). The letters *d* and *r*, on which the textual question pivots, are closely alike in Hebrew.

[7] The Heb. text has 'They turn not upward' (*lō' 'āl*), an unusual expression both in word order and in meaning (since *'al* is normally a preposition, 'on', 'over', etc.). Some versions therefore assume a copying error for *lĕba'al*, 'to Baal' (see RSV; but cf. NIV, NRSV). Yet the modern name El Al ('to the height'), adopted by the Israelis for their airline, is a reminder that a noun ('height') underlies the preposition; and indeed *'el 'al* occurs in the Heb. of 11:7, on which see note. On balance, however, the conjectured reading 'to Baal' seems the most likely.

section, pp. 58ff.) It is perhaps the most serious of the four, for a weapon may imply a life-and-death situation, in which its failure spells the end of everything. And this *faulty bow* is not merely weak: it is warped, as the context of 'speaking falsely' and 'plotting evil' makes clear. Psalm 78:57 puts it well:

> Like their ancestors they were disloyal and faithless,
>> as unreliable as a faulty bow.

O Lord, grant us grace never to parley with temptation, never to tamper with conscience, never to spare the right eye, or hand, or foot that is a snare to us; never to lose our souls, though in exchange we should gain the whole world.
(Christina Rossetti)

Hosea 8:1–14

10. Sowing the wind, reaping the whirlwind

If there is one theme that unifies the diversity of this chapter, it is that of Israel's dangerous self-reliance, with its self-appointed kings, its man-made calf, its expensive allies, its own version of religion, and its impressive fortresses. What God makes of all this, and what kind of test it could survive, these people have not troubled to ask themselves.

1. Alarmist or realist? (8:1–3)

If no-one in Hosea's day, gazing complacently at the house or household of the Lord (like the disciples admiring the temple in Matt. 24:1), had noticed the ominous speck in the sky above it, it was high time someone pointed it out. The eagle[1] might not have long to wait; the object of its interest, the ailing nation, had even less. Its plight was nearly too late to mend. The Hebrew of verse 1 raps out the command in three words: 'Trumpet to your-lips!'

Yet nobody could quite believe it. We sense their mood as the chapter unfolds. 'Yes, times are bad, but surely not desperate! Another coup – who knows? – may bring the right man to the top. Abroad, we are bidding high for allies. Religion? There at least we are strong. Defence? We have a fine building programme. Let's at least be cheerful!' (cf. 9:1).

---

[1] There is a slight query over this word, which is qualified by the particle 'as' (see RSV mg.). On the basis of an Arabic word of similar consonants, Grace Emmerson offers the translation 'lips, as a herald [making a proclamation] against the house of the Lord' (*VT* 25 [1975], pp. 700–710). But the expression, lit. 'as-an-eagle', can be defended as indicating that the prophet is not speaking literally: cf. the repetitions of 'like' (the same particle) in Ezek. 1:26f.

The cry of verse 2, *Our God, we acknowledge* [or 'know'] *you!*, has the double reliance on birth and breeding which would show itself again in the Jews' disputes with Jesus. 'We are Abraham's descendants'; 'We are disciples of Moses! *We know* . . .' (John 8:33; 9:28f.). The divine reply is virtually the same in both instances: your actions drown your words (see, e.g., John 8:39–44, 55). And in case we point the finger too easily at proud Israelites and Jews, the same test is applied to us: 'Whoever says, "I know him," but does not do what he commands is a liar' (1 John 2:4).

What may seem at first merely repetitive in the triple accusation of verses 1–3 is in fact triply devastating, for the *covenant* spoke of the basic relationship with God – as binding and as intimate as marriage; the *law* spelt out the ways in which alone that partnership could be harmonious; and *what is good* covers not only all this but everything that conscience and plain decency demand, or even that common sense suggests – for 'good' is by definition not only what is worth doing but what is worth having and worth being. To spurn this is to fall for a bargain that is no bargain – to 'spend' (as Isa. 55:2 has put it)

> money on what is not bread,
>> and your labour on what does not satisfy

– and, we might add, 'your life for certain death'.

2. The self-help that is no help (8:4–14)

The rest of the chapter pursues the theme launched in the first word of verse 4: '*They* set up kings . . .' – for the Hebrew makes the 'They' emphatic here. Everything that follows has this pattern of 'They . . . but not through me' (see NRSV), whether it is politics, religion, diplomacy or defence.

a. Puppet kings and puppet gods (8:4–6)

The classic comment on 'not through me' and *without my approval* (i.e. my recognition) is Psalm 127: 'Unless the LORD builds the house . . . Unless the LORD watches over the city . . . [It is] in vain.' This disastrous kingmaking was part of a long series in Scripture, starting as far back as Abimelek, that 'thorn-bush' fit only to start a forest fire (Judg. 9:15), and reaching its spiritual climax in the cry, 'No, not him! Give us Barabbas!' (John 18:40). That cry is echoed wherever the voice of the people (our vaunted democracy) drowns the voice of God; where we set up leaders and regimes supposedly answerable only to ourselves; where we treat even the moral law as subject to the vote or to the climate of opinion.

Although the kingmaking castigated here was far from democratic in our sense – being a series of conspiracies and bloody coups[2] – God saw it as the people's doing for all that; for the violence at the top had its roots in the anarchy below. We could have guessed as much, but 4:1–3 has already put it beyond doubt.

Next, the puppet gods. The golden calf, or young bull, as a man-made god, had an even longer past for Israel than the man-made king. Its famous first appearance was, outrageously, at the foot of Mount Sinai itself and at the instigation of the future high priest, Aaron (Exod. 32:1ff.). (Perhaps by now we should be less surprised than Moses, though no less scandalized, at the high patronage that heresy has a way of securing from time to time.) Later, just after Solomon, Jeroboam I set up two golden calves, one at Bethel and one at Dan, as rallying points for his breakaway kingdom of the north, Hosea's native land, as counter-attractions to the temple at Jerusalem (1 Kgs 12:27–30).

To us, a golden calf may seem completely unconvincing. But an accepted superstition, rather like an established point of etiquette, can put almost anything beyond challenge, bypassing reason even when reason utterly explodes it, as Hosea's argument does here.[3] In addition, though, it probably reflected an element of pagan thinking, since a bull is an obvious symbol of brute strength and sexual potency – qualities a corrupt society tends to idolize. In that case, ancient Israel and Canaan may be closer to us than we suppose.

There is a telling link between verses 3 and 5 in the strong word translated 'spurned' in the RSV (NIV *rejected . . . throw out*):

Israel has spurned the good . . .
I have spurned your calf, O Samar'ia

---

[2] See above, p. 58.

[3] W. F. Albright's contention (*From the Stone Age to Christianity* [Doubleday Anchor Books, 1957], p. 299) that the calf was regarded as a mere pedestal for the invisible Yahweh (an idea based on Canaanite representations of the storm-god standing on a bull) would make the argument of verse 6 quite pointless. But Hosea knew his countrymen's beliefs too well to waste irrelevant ammunition on them. Clearly they were treating the calves as divine. Cf. 13:2.

– although the RSV has trimmed the second of these from a literal 'he has' to 'I have', to make a smoother fit with the surrounding 'me' and 'my' (see RSV mg.). Either way, it is a sharp reminder that our lordly choices are not the last word in any situation. There is another will, another verdict, to be reckoned with.

But it may be an appeal: *Throw out your calf-idol, Samaria!*[4] – for there is once again a divine yearning in verse 5 (*How long . . . ?*) mingled with the anger.

b. Desperate diplomacy (8:7–10)[5]

Sow the wind and reap the whirlwind has become so much a part of our language that we may miss the surprise of it here. Hearing it for the first time, we should expect the reaping to be simply negative: 'put nothing in, and you'll get nothing out'. Instead, the harvest is positive disaster, as in Paul's sequence: 'Whoever sows to please their flesh, from the flesh will reap' – not disappointment, but 'destruction' (Gal. 6:8) – for there are no half measures in the end.

The main context here is foreign policy, but the main issue is faith – and fidelity. As the last chapter showed (7:11ff.), Israel was gambling on one hunch after another, forever changing sides and (as our verse 10 points out) desperately bidding for influential friendships. This way she would win only distrust and scorn as *something no one wants*, or as NRSV puts it, 'a useless vessel'; and in the end she would reap the terrible fate of a traitor. So the metaphorical harvest – the whirlwind of judgment – would be accompanied by quite literally empty fields, either as the fertility cult of Baal failed its devotees (see 7a–b, with 2:5, 9), or as the punitive armies stripped the land (7c).

The lesson needs no spiritualizing to bring it to our doorstep. Certainly it is valid at the spiritual level, as Galatians 6 points out, for false religion pays disastrous dividends. But guile and duplicity in any field, political, commercial or personal, are equally perilous tactics to adopt. Dabbling in evil, we may be amateurs; but we are playing with professionals who will make short work of us, as we are warned not only in the well-known saying of Ephesians 6:12 ('For our struggle is not against flesh and blood, but

---

[4] NIV, following LXX, reading the existing consonants with a shortened first vowel. (NEB opts for a similar but rare verb, 'to stink', in both verses – a more precarious translation.)

[5] In 10b RSV follows LXX. The NIV (cf. also NRSV, RV) is preferable here in retaining the Masoretic Text, which it renders, *They will begin to waste away under the oppression of the mighty king* (lit. 'a king of princes').

against the rulers, against the authorities, against the powers of this dark world and against the spiritual forces of evil') but in the detailed admonitions that lead up to it from Ephesians 4:25 onwards.

c. Religiosity (8:11–13)

The first two lines of this read so oddly, as they stand, that most modern versions have taken a fresh look at the Hebrew consonants to see if they will yield a better meaning. (The original text, like modern Hebrew, left the reader to supply the vowels.) The NIV (cf. GNB) offers as good a solution as any, keeping the consonants unchanged but pronouncing them so as to read: *altars for sin offerings . . . have become altars for sinning.*[6]

This chimes in forcefully with verse 13 and with the protests of Hosea's contemporaries, Amos, Micah and Isaiah (e.g. Amos 5:21ff.; Mic. 6:6ff.; Isa. 1:11ff.). Paul had to warn us of something very similar (1 Cor. 11:27). It seems to be an occupational disease of worshippers to think more of the mechanics than the meaning of what we do; more of getting it right than of getting ourselves right; and this can degenerate from thoughtlessness into something worse, ranging from cynical detachment, if we are sophisticated, to religious superstition if we are not. What the prophets show us is heaven's strong reaction to such attitudes: that this parody of worship is not simply valueless, as we might have guessed, but insulting and even sickening to God, attracting the very judgment it is supposed to avert. This is the irony that runs throughout this paragraph. It is put more vehemently still in the invective of Isaiah and Amos, in the passages we have noted, and above all in the shuddering words of Christ to lukewarm Laodicea (Rev. 3:16).

The gulf between such worshippers and God is seen at its widest in verse 12. There is no meeting of minds, divine and human; still less of wills. This verse, incidentally, has been a talking point between critical scholars on the question of how much or little of God's law was in writing in Hosea's day;[7] but its real aim is to show how deaf to all appeal and all

---

[6] I.e. reading the intensive (Pi'el) form of 'to sin' in 11a, and the non-intensive (Qal) in 11b. The Pi'el form means to make a sin offering; the Qal, using the same consonants, means to sin. (Note that English, like Hebrew, sometimes uses the same verb to mean either the doing or the undoing of a thing: e.g. we 'dust' an object with a powder, or dust it clean; and so on.)

[7] On their own showing, God's laws had been in writing since the days of Moses (Exod. 24:3–7; Deut. 31:24–26). If confirmation were needed, the AV of Hos. 8:12 ('I have written . . .') would seem to supply it (cf. NIV), but the Heb. construction tends to favour a hypothetical statement, as in RSV etc., or a present tense: 'I write down countless teachings' (GNB; cf. NEB).

correction God's people have become. However much he says, and however plainly (for it is given as written law), it will be treated as an irrelevance or a kind of incantation, while the services and sacraments (as in 13a) continue and proliferate. The New Testament reports the same shutting of the mind to the gospel as to the law (e.g. Matt. 13:13ff. and parallels; John 12:37ff.; Acts 28:25ff.), and reveals the source, deep in our fallen nature, of this deafness to the voice of God: 'The natural man receiveth not the things of the Spirit of God: for they are foolishness unto him: neither can he know them, because they are spiritually discerned' (1 Cor. 2:14, AV).

In the threat *they will return to Egypt* (13), perhaps the deepest thrust lies in the word *return*. Was *this* to be the end of their great epic, the exodus? Elsewhere Assyria is coupled with Egypt as their place of exile, and Assyria was in fact to be their conqueror and captor; so Egypt probably received only refugees. Yet this word 'return' is used in 9:3 and 11:5 as well as here, for they had spiritually retraced their steps to Egypt long before they did so physically. It stands in pointed contrast to the couplet of 11:1:

> When Israel was a child, I loved him,
> and out of Egypt I called my son.

Even so, the last word would be with grace, not judgment:

> They will come from Egypt,
> trembling like sparrows,
> from Assyria, fluttering like doves.
> (11:11)

In these and other references to their oldest captivity, the pattern of the book, as *grace – disgrace – grace abounding*, comes out once more.

d. Misplaced trust (8:14)

The first sentence of this is the key to it, for the Old Testament does not despise fine buildings or strong walls (cf. Ps. 48:12–13, but 14): only the notion that they are in themselves fit to be one's glory[8] or security. Nehemiah, building his wall and carefully deploying his little workforce, showed the right priorities in his order of the day: '*Remember the Lord,*

---

[8] See the scathing comment on Jehoiakim's palace in Jer. 22:13–17.

who is great and awesome, and fight for your families, your sons and your daughters, your wives and your homes' (Neh. 4:14).

As for Judah's *fortified . . . towns*, the brutal answer to them was only a generation away. There were forty-six of them, according to Sennacherib, and their fate is told in a single verse of 2 Kings. 'In the fourteenth year of King Hezekiah's reign, Sennacherib king of Assyria attacked all the fortified cities of Judah and captured them' (2 Kgs 18:13). The only one to survive was Jerusalem, following the message from God to Hezekiah which opened with the significant words: 'I have heard your prayer concerning Sennacherib king of Assyria' (2 Kgs 19:20).

Hosea 9:1–17

11. Wanderers among the nations

The sentencing of Israel to a wandering existence, in the final verse, will round off a chapter which has fully paved the way to it. This people has been restless enough, ogling one nation after another; heedless enough, dismissing as madmen its lookout men, the prophets; fickle enough, forsaking the Lord for Baal even from the days of Moses. Hosea will increasingly draw on history in the next few chapters, chiefly with passing allusions, to show how well earned are the judgments he is having to pronounce from God.

1. The party is over (9:1–6)

To us in our secular age it may seem odd that God should expect *religious* warnings to have much impact on a set of people as far gone in sin as Israel was. *Briers* submerging their treasures, yes; and *thorns* taking over their deserted dwellings (6): these were a prospect to shake the most hardened. But ritually forbidden food (3c)? Cessation of sacrifice (4)? No pilgrimages (5)? How could these be matters for dismay?

The clue is in the previous chapter, at 8:12–13; and above all in chapter 2. Religion, to them, penetrated everything except the conscience. It was a charm against trouble, a compelling pattern of festivals, stories, customs and taboos that gave shape to life; and with its heady Canaanite embellishments it could have the excitement of an orgy. It also gave you an identity: you, your people, your traditions, your native soil and the God or gods who presided over your land – all these were a close-knit structure whose disintegration would leave you totally adrift.

The one thing missing was the very heart of true religion, the loyal love that alone could make God's covenant partner a true wife to him. As it was, his will held not the slightest interest for her, as 8:12 showed; her only loyalty was to her appetites. The harsh word *prostitute* (9:1) was no exaggeration. And in case our interest in the portrait should be only academic, as if it were applicable solely to ancient idolaters or, at most, modern renegades, the New Testament startles us with a similar outburst in James 4:4 against mere worldliness – calling us in that case 'adulterers and adulteresses', although some modern versions have put it more politely.

Israel's judgment would be all too fitting. For her political flirtations she would have her fill of foreign loves, her people captive in Assyria and fugitives in Egypt.[1] For her religious flirtations, too, she would pay the proper price of having scattered her favours everywhere: her people ending up with nothing fit to offer God, and nowhere to hold their beloved festivals.[2]

2. 'The prophet is a fool' (9:7–9)

When disembodied fingers wrote an unintelligible message at Belshazzar's feast, the king was sobered at once, and desperate for an answer (Dan. 5:5ff.). But when a man of God spoke intelligibly and with passion to his own people, he was *a fool* and *a maniac* (7). He was not the first or last to be called this. 'Why did this maniac come to you?' was the reaction of Jehu's friends to a prophet's visit; and Jeremiah was named in a letter which urged the authorities to put 'any maniac who acts like a prophet into the stocks and neck-irons' (see 2 Kgs 9:11; Jer. 29:26–27). Paul was to be paid the same compliment by Festus (Acts 26:24), and our Lord was accused of being demon-possessed (John 7:20; 8:48).

Jesus told us to expect and welcome a prophet's persecution and misrepresentation (Matt. 5:12); and here verse 8b gives a sample of such treatment in the attempts to entangle and compromise the speaker (the *snares*) and in the special venom of religious disdain (*hostility in the house of his God*). What Hosea lets us glimpse in this single sentence, Jeremiah

---

[1] See verse 3, and the comment on 'they will return to Egypt' at 8:13.

[2] The point of the comparison with *the bread of mourners* is not that one ate forbidden food on such occasions, but that mourning rites made one technically unclean by their association with death; and it was sacrilege to partake of holy things while so disqualified (see Deut. 26:14; Lev. 7:21). Just so, the defilement of heathen Assyria would cling to them all the time that they were there under judgment.

reveals to us at length, recording the threats to his life by his fellow villagers (Jer. 11:19, 21), the taunts and whisperings (Jer. 17:15ff.; 20:10), the isolation: 'I sat alone because your hand was on me' (Jer. 15:17). But God, in our passage, has a better name than 'fool' for such a man: *The prophet . . . is the watchman* (8) – a calling whose implications can be studied in some detail in Ezekiel 33:1–9.

While rejection is a prophet's honour, it is a people's doom. This judgment is expressed impersonally at the beginning of this paragraph (7a), as a due process of law (*punishment*) and a settling of accounts ('recompense', NRSV; *reckoning*, NIV), but in personal terms in the closing statement (9b), where the Lord himself exacts the penalty. These two aspects of judgment, as the inexorable logic of events and as the act of God in person, are held together in Scripture. The couplet

God will remember their wickedness
    and punish them for their sins

is the dark alternative to the grace of the new covenant, which is equally personal:

I will forgive their wickedness
    and will remember their sins no more.
    (Jer. 31:34)

There is no middle way, and no sidestepping of repentance if grace is to prevail.

As for the depth of Israel's guilt, the mere mention of *Gibeah* (9) is measurement enough, for its story in Judges 19 – 21 leaves Sodom and Gomorrah with nothing they could teach this city, whose depravity at that period was equalled only by its arrogance in brazening the matter out. For a fuller treatment of such moral value reversals we have Paul's study in Romans 1:18–32, where his final comment (32) could as readily have arisen from an encounter with our present society as with his own or with Hosea's.

3. The glory departs (9:10–14)

Delight and anticipation could hardly be more vividly expressed than in this opening reminiscence of the Lord's great early venture with his people. Allowing for its language of relish and dreamlike anomaly – *grapes in the desert!* – the passage conveys something our careful theology cannot quite pin down: the Lord's zest and enjoyment, so different from cold charity, in his encounters with responsive love, however meagre that response may be.

It makes the shock of disappointment all the stronger – and this again is something our consciousness of divine foreknowledge and of measured wrath may hide from us. But in the Gospels the echo of verse 10a in the incident of the barren fig tree, so eagerly approached at a moment of hunger (Matt. 21:18ff.), makes the same point about God and humanity, at whatever risk of pricking us into high-minded protest.

The story of Baal Peor (10b), which can be read in Numbers 25, is very apt, since it combined the two kinds of unchastity Hosea had to fight: the physical and the spiritual. It was not only the Moabite women but their local Baal that had seduced the men of the exodus; and we have already heard Hosea's protests against the same two levels of adultery in his day (e.g. 2:13; 4:14). We might add that in our own day the virtual worshipping of sex, needing no Baal to make it a religion, has proved as potent a distraction as it was in Old Testament times. Incidentally Hosea is not being merely rhetorical when he calls apostates *as vile as the thing they loved.* Using a standard term for idols, namely, 'thing of shame' (NRSV; NIV *shameful idol*), he points out that what you give yourself to, you not only come to resemble (Ps. 115:8), but you make common cause with it. If it is an abomination to God, so, appallingly, are you; if its second name is 'shame',[3] so is yours.

What follows from this allusion to Baal Peor and the surrender to lust is not a set of arbitrary punishments but the end products of so squalid and treacherous a choice. The quickest thing to disappear, when this fever grips a people, is *glory* (11) – whether in the sense of self-respect (for conscience must be silenced by cynicism), or of reputation, or, more profoundly, of the glory of God's presence. A nation may be spiritless enough to shrug off the loss of glory, but what is left *when I* [the LORD] *turn away from them* (12)? The name Ichabod marked such a moment, or so at least it seemed, in an earlier generation, when the ark of God was captured (1 Sam. 4:21); and Ezekiel would later have a vision of God's glory withdrawing from Jerusalem (Ezek. 8:6; 11:23). For our comfort we can

---

[3] In the Heb. text, 'Bosheth', i.e. 'shame', is a frequent substitute for 'Baal' in the Old Testament (cf. RSV).

remember the sequel to that capture and, in Ezekiel 43:2ff., to that withdrawal; but the people whom Hosea was addressing would soon be losing not only their glory but their corporate identity as the northern kingdom, for ever.

But whether or not they cared about the loss of glory or of God, there was another and more tangible loss to face. From verse 11 to the end of the chapter the family tree of Ephraim (that is, of the northern tribes) is seen either dying back or being lopped of all new growth. They have worshipped fertility through the sex rites of Baal, and they have sold their souls for peace (see, e.g., 7:11; 8:9f.): their judgment will be infertility and war. Here again it is a blend of natural and supernatural processes: natural, in that in any case the abuse of sex tends towards disease and to the barrenness of 11b and 14, and that broken treaties tend to leave a country friendless (12–13);[4] but supernatural in that God will see this matter through to the bitter end.

4. The disinherited (9:15–17)

Every nation has its celebrated spots whose names evoke the glories of the past or present. Yet sometimes it might be startling to compare their earthly with their heavenly reputations. Gilgal is a case in point: hallowed by its altars (12:11) and its famous names and moments (Joshua's first foothold in the Promised Land, Saul's first kingly glory, David's welcome back from exile; Josh. 4:19; 1 Sam. 11:14–15; 2 Sam. 19:15) – all of which leave God entirely unimpressed. Far from hallowed, it is crammed with evil; and the only reference to its history (if such it is in verse 15a) is to its role in forfeiting God's favour for the nation as a whole.

In its direct, outspoken way this is as devastating as Amos's barbed mockery of its corrupted shrine and superstitious pilgrims:

Go to Bethel and sin;
    go to Gilgal and sin yet more.
(Amos 4:4)

But what is meant by *I hated them there*? 'Hate' is a harsh Hebrew way of expressing rejection, used with varying degrees of severity and emotional

---

4 RSV and some modern versions follow LXX in 13a, but the Heb. text is as in NIV: *I have seen Ephraim, like Tyre, planted in a pleasant place. But* . . .

content.[5] The warm affection which pervades this book from end to end (see, e.g., 3:1b; 11:1ff.; 14:4) forbids us to take either *I hated them there* or *I will no longer love them* (15) as an expression of mere animosity. Rather this language is announcing (with what anguish, other passages make evident: e.g. 6:4; 11:8) a break-off in relations which amounts to the suspension of the marriage (*I will drive them out of my house,* 15) as the only hope of mending it. The theme has already met us in the sequence of severity and tenderness in 2:2ff. with 2:14ff. and in the last verse of chapter 5.

Incidentally the NRSV is somewhat misleading here, since the Hebrew of verse 15a does not say 'there I *came to* hate them', as though God had taken a sudden and growing dislike to them at this place. Gilgal, for whatever reason, marked a climax rather than a beginning of these strained relations. If, as some think, the reference is to Israel's first clamour for a king – certainly a theme in Hosea: for example, 13:9–11 – that confrontation in fact took place at Ramah (1 Sam. 8:4–9), not Gilgal (1 Sam. 11:12–15). So it seems more likely that the special sin of Gilgal lay in the flagrantly false worship – false by its immorality, hypocrisy and heresy (cf. 4:14–19) – which evidently flourished there even more than in its fellow sanctuaries at Bethel and elsewhere.

So the chapter ends with a reiteration of the nation's immediate prospect, which was equally God's sentence and their own choice; a fourfold doom of barrenness, carnage, estrangement and homelessness. The last of these, *they will be wanderers among the nations,* was to become, tragically, part of their distinctive and proverbial reputation – yet it was not the last word that God would have for them. For this, see Romans 11 in its entirety, but especially verses 11–16 and 25 to the end.

---

[5] The discipleship sayings, e.g. Luke 14:26, are at one extreme, and that of 1 John 3:15 at the other. A non-emotional example is the birth oracle on Jacob and Esau as expressed in Rom. 9:12–13. An emotional equivalent of 'love less than' is in Gen. 29:31 with 30; and of either this or 'dislike' in Deut. 21:15–17.

Hosea 10:1–15

12. 'Time to seek the Lord'

There is great variety in this chapter, for all its insistence on a single theme of warning. It draws now on early history (9), now on more recent memories (14); it bombards us with lively metaphors (4, 7, 11), ominous predictions (7–8), common-sense logic (13), snatches of current talk (3); it is always changing its angle of attack. But its thrust is positive: to spur readers, not to stun them. The one gleam of light, the invitation of verse 12, is the *raison d'être* of the whole chapter.

1. Bounty and betrayal (10:1–2)

When Jesus said, 'I am the true vine' (John 15:1ff.), the vine of Israel was the background to his words – this favoured and once flourishing but ever disappointing specimen, whose promise and purpose he alone was fit to fulfil. As for Israel (and as for us, the true vine's branches?), the more God did for them the more they misapplied it. Isaiah 5:1–7 follows the metaphor through, to speak of Israel's 'bad fruit' of violence and injustice; and Hosea did much the same in the previous chapter (9:10ff.), with his picture of their forebears as fruit that had rapidly gone rotten.

Now he uses it more freely, passing on to the literal fruitfulness of their land – God's gift – and the offensive crop of altars and pillars – the people's wrong-headed response – that kept pace with this prosperity. Chapter 2 has already given us the clue to God's anger at this, for these were not only a material instead of a spiritual response: they were the paraphernalia of Baal worship, thinly disguised as worship of the Lord; and their prime object was to insure against lean times. As J. L. Mays has caustically remarked, 'the development of cultic sanctuaries was simply turning part of the profit back into the business. Altars and pillars were the holy machinery which produced the prosperity – a typically Canaanite understanding of cult.'[1]

Typically Canaanite, to be sure; and we may add, for our own instruction, typically carnal, not only in its calculating attitude to God but in its obsession with externals and its quickness to absorb the spirit of the surrounding culture. 'The more God did for them' (we might say about our own ecclesiastical record), 'the more structures they set up and the more they merged with their environment.'

2. Disenchantment (10:3–6)

We might well wonder whether arrogance or apathy is the greater of two evils for a nation. For Israel, the mood had swung between the two, marked by their changing attitudes towards the throne: at one moment pinning all their hopes to kingship ('Give me a king and princes', 13:10); at another cheapening it with debauchery and tearing it apart with assassinations (7:3–7); finally, here in verse 3, shrugging it off as meaningless, along with everything else, from the Lord downwards. Only their superstition, their talisman the golden calf, will awaken any sense of loss by its removal.

When heaven is considered empty (*we did not revere the Lord*, 3), words and promises soon follow suit, and justice, so-called, becomes a parody of its true self – no longer towering impartially above the strong and the weak, but earthbound and tortuous, springing from the thoughts and policies of the moment; no longer a force for good and for the nation's health, but a source of poison. The picture of it as a weed which takes over a farmer's field (4) provides a startling contrast to the majestic metaphors of height and depth and clarity associated with true, divine justice ('on high, out of . . . sight', Ps. 10:5, NRSV; 'like the great deep', Ps. 36:6; 'like the sun', Hos. 6:5).[2] The accusation is borne out by history. At best, humanism takes its estimate of morality and justice from ground level – from whatever happens to be a society's current mood and practice; while at

---

[1] Mays, p. 139.

[2] I understand 'judgment' here (4, RSV) in the prevailing OT sense of the 'justice' (cf. GNB) dispensed by a judge or practised as morality between one person and another. But it may have here its further meaning of punishment, or again (as in NEB, NRSV; cf. NIV), litigation.

worst, tyrants and demagogues equate it simply with their policies and interests. So the false morality strengthens its hold on the community, choking the true values as a wild crop smothers the good growth under its spreading carpet.

It is hardly surprising that the paragraph ends by predicting a typically confused human state of mind in verses 5 and 6: a sense of vanished glory, appropriately enough, yet attached to the very thing that was the nation's shame, the calf of Bethel.[3] In Samuel's day (as we saw in chapter 9 with the comments on verse 11) the captured ark of God had been lamented, as well it might be; but now Israel's tears will be for a captured idol and symbol of apostasy – for Jeroboam I had set it up at Bethel to create a rival cult against Jerusalem (1 Kgs 12:26–33). This is the mourning that springs from disappointment and wounded pride rather than repentance; a 'worldly sorrow' that leads nowhere, rather than the godly sorrow that 'leads to salvation and leaves no regret' (cf. 2 Cor. 7:10).

As a postscript to the passage, notice the expression *the great king* (6), which has already met us at 5:13. Such was a title of the Assyrian monarchs; but the Hebrew text gives it a scornful twist, to read 'king Jareb' (AV, RV), 'a king who will contend' (cf. NRSV mg.). George Adam Smith found the perfect equivalent: 'King Pick-Quarrel'.[4] In a single word Hosea has shown up the hopelessness of attempting to buy off so inveterate an aggressor.

3. Days of reckoning (10:7–10)

There is never a lack of lively imagery in this book. Here, in the space of the first two verses, three very different pictures put a rapid end to thoughts of human self-sufficiency. The king 'under whose shadow [we thought] we would live among the nations' (cf. Lam. 4:20)[5] would prove to be no massive oak, deep-rooted and reassuring, but a *twig on the surface of a torrent*, overtaken by events and whisked helplessly away. If that picture is all turbulence, the next one, of shrines and altars deserted and overgrown, is ominously still. Added to this, the nickname 'Aven' (the

---

[3] Once again, as in 4:15, Bethel ('house of God') is renamed Beth Aven, 'house of iniquity'. Cf. verse 8, where it is simply 'Aven' (see, e.g., NRSV).

[4] Smith, pp. 263, 287.

[5] Although these words refer to the Davidic king of Judah, they express something of the exalted view of kingship that was current at the time, as 13:10 implies.

word translated as *wickedness* in NIV) for these holy places and the comment that they are *the sin of Israel* together say the last word on man-made religion. But the last word on human arrogance and independence is reserved for the end of the verse: *they will say to the mountains, 'Cover us!'* – a cry which the New Testament will take up twice: first to predict the still greater horrors awaiting the Jerusalem of AD 70 as the logical outcome of its Good Friday choice; and second to portray the terrors of the Last Judgment, with people of every rank and nation calling 'to the mountains and the rocks, "Fall on us and hide us from the face of him who sits on the throne and from the wrath of the Lamb!"' (Luke 23:30; Rev. 6:16).

So we are not left to contemplate the downfall of Samaria[6] on its own, safely isolated in the eighth century BC. It meets us as a foretaste of still weightier events, as indeed are all the local, limited tragedies of history. Our Lord laid down for us the right and wrong reactions to such happenings when he was asked to comment on a massacre:

> Do you think that these Galileans were worse sinners than all the other Galileans because they suffered this way? I tell you, no! But unless you repent, you too will all perish. Or those eighteen who died when the tower in Siloam fell on them – do you think they were more guilty than all the others living in Jerusalem? I tell you, no! But unless you repent, you too will all perish.
> (Luke 13:2–5)

We can hardly complain that the last act of our human drama has been under-rehearsed!

Once more, as so often in these closing chapters, God now reinforces what he has to say with a reminder of past history. The name Gibeah (9) is doubly potent, linking Hosea's generation with the most vicious episode in Israel's past (see the comments on 9:9) and with its aftermath, the destructive civil war of Judges 20. But verse 10 appoints foreign nations, not fellow Israelites this time, as the means of punishment. The fulfilment is recorded in 2 Kings 17:6 and, for good measure, 24–41.

Before we pass on from verse 10, two details may be worth pointing out. First, the opening line in the Hebrew text reads simply, 'At my desire

---

[6] See the map on p. 106 and the diagram on pp. 107ff.

(i.e. when I so decide) I will chastise them.'[7] Second, the last line reads 'to bind them to their two sins'. If this is right (but 'bind' could be a copying error for the similar word 'chastise'), it makes two points about the judgment that must fall: first, that it awaits God's chosen time; and second, that it ties the sinner to the sinner's choice. Nothing could be less fortuitous or less arbitrary.

As for the *double sin*, many suggested meanings have been offered. Among the most likely is that it refers to Israel's resort to Baal in its worship and to worldly allies in its politics – both of which are major accusations in these chapters. Another is that the allusion is to their rejection first of God as their true king and then of David as his anointed. This double defection is implied in 3:5, but that passage is hardly close at hand here. Further suggestions fasten on the reference to Gibeah just before this, and see the two sins either as those of Israel's past and present, or else as the outrage of Judges 19 plus the disobedient reign of Saul (who made Gibeah his centre). Some of these interpretations seem over-subtle, and it may be that the simplest of all should be followed: that like the 'three sins . . . even . . . four' of Amos 1:3, 6, and so on, the two iniquities mean just the repeated or persistent acts of Israel's disobedience.

4. A choice of harvests (10:11–15)

This is very typical of Hosea's preaching, with its glance back to a happier past (11a), its resourceful use of metaphors – here drawn from farming – and its conclusion in unmistakably plain speaking.

The point about the heifer in the opening verse (11) is that threshing was a comparatively light task, made pleasant by the fact that the creature was unmuzzled and free to eat (Deut. 25:4) as it pulled the threshing-sledge over the gathered corn. This owner's pride in his beast, and his consideration for it (cf. Prov. 12:10), together with the creature's obedience and contentment, provides one of the many affectionate touches in these troubled chapters.

But the idyllic scene had to change. Perhaps we are meant to see that in any case there must be a transition to hard and testing work, in any worthwhile enterprise and for any growth to maturity:

---

[7] NRSV's longer first line, 'I will come against the wayward people to punish them', is an adaptation of the LXX of verses 9b–10a.

> Son though he was, he learned obedience from what he suffered . . .
> because the Lord disciplines the one he loves.
> (Heb. 5:8; 12:6)

But in Israel's case (and Judah's, 11b) the hardship was compounded by her retreat into obstinacy. 'The Israelites are stubborn, like a stubborn heifer' (4:16). So the yoke of verse 11 would no longer be the well-fitting one of God's ideal design, but the harsh, heavy collar of slavery. What would be said one day of Babylon and Judah would be doubly true of Assyria and Ephraim:

> I gave them into your hand,
>   and you showed them no mercy.
> Even on the aged
>   you laid a very heavy yoke.
> (Isa. 47:6)

Yet the picture is not one of unrelieved or pointless gloom. The yoke, after all, is there to serve the best of ends, the harvest, through the best of means, the plough and harrow. So verse 12a is as positive as it is practical, and 12b as generous as it is urgent. The expression 'unploughed ground' was extraordinarily well suited to describe a people doubly impervious to the good seed of God's word, both by the tangled growth of worldly notions and preoccupations which had taken hold of them, and by the hard crust beneath it all, of wills and attitudes never broken into penitence.

A later prophet was to take this up and spell it out with the call, 'Break up your unploughed ground, and do not sow among thorns' (Jer. 4:3); and still the parable of the Sower (Matt. 13) speaks to such a situation, forbidding us to confine Hosea's challenge simply to his own generation. As for his urgent conclusion, *it is time to seek the Lord* (12), certainly we can see with hindsight just how little time was left for Israel, whose kingdom fell almost before Hosea had finished speaking. But again it is a warning that speaks today – indeed, as Hebrews 3:13 puts it, 'encourage one another daily, as long as it is called "Today"' – since the present is the only time that lies to hand, with the past beyond recall and the future beyond conjecture.

With verse 13 the warning note returns, to mount to a new climax. First it takes up the metaphors of the plough, the harvest and the table, this time to highlight the iron chain of causality between them. In verse 12 it was a golden chain, leading to *the fruit of unfailing love*[8] as surely as this one leads to *the fruit of deception* (13). What such fruit consists of – in a word, the breakdown of all sound relationships and the corrupting of all values – is pictured poetically in the 'grapes . . . filled with poison' of Deuteronomy 32:32, and expounded in unsparing detail in Isaiah 59:1–15. For another and more famous saying of Hosea on sowing and reaping, see 8:7 and the comment there.

But the metaphors now give way to stark, literal reality; and the charge of injustice and treachery is supplemented by that of military jingoism as the chapter ends. It hardly matters that we can only guess at the identities of *Shalman* and *Beth Arbel*,[9] for we can gather what those names meant to Hosea's first hearers: names as horrific to them as 'Hitler' and 'Belsen' to us. Yet, to make it worse, a conqueror's atrocities against mothers and children (14b) were clearly all too common (see 2 Kgs 8:12; 15:16; Ps. 137:8–9; Isa. 13:16; Amos 1:13; Nah. 3:10), even if an extra ruthlessness or the force of an event fresh in the memory added a special sharpness to the present warning. Any romantic eagerness we may feel towards military or revolutionary adventures should be chilled by our contemplating the sequence of 'Because . . . therefore . . .' in 13b, 14a (NRSV) and of *as . . . So . . .* in 14b, 15a.

There is no need to 'correct' the final sentence so as to open with the words 'In the storm' (RSV, JB).[10] The existing text makes perfectly good sense as *When that day dawns* or, more freely, 'As sure as day dawns' (NEB). It shows that the king can no more postpone the day of reckoning than he could stem the torrent of verse 7 that was to sweep him away.

---

[8] The LXX reads 'the fruit of' (Heb. *pĕrî*) in verse 12, matching the expression of verse 13. The Masoretic Text, however, has 'according to' (*lĕpî*) in verse 12.

[9] Shalman is most probably short for Shalmaneser of Assyria: either Shalmaneser V (727–722 BC), whose march to besiege Samaria could well have taken him through Beth Arbel (? the Arbela of 1 Macc. 9:2, near the west shore of the lake of Galilee); or alternatively Shalmaneser III of the previous century (859–824 BC), who campaigned against Syria (Aram), Hauran and Israel in 841 BC, and whose route could well have included this Arbela or another Arbela near Pella, east of the Jordan. See M. Astour, 'The First Assyrian Invasion of Israel', *JAOS* 91 (1971), pp. 386f. for the latter view; but more cautiously, M. Elat in *IEJ* 25 (1975), p. 31, note 25.

[10] I.e. to substitute a conjectured *śaʿar*, 'storm', for *šaḥar*, 'dawn'.

Hosea 11:1–11

13. 'How can I give you up?'

This chapter is one of the boldest in the Old Testament – indeed in the whole Bible – in exposing to us the mind and heart of God in human terms. We are always in danger of thinking of divine majesty in terms we have learnt from earthly potentates, 'the kings of the Gentiles' whom our Lord summed up in Luke 22:25–27 in contrast to himself. Even when we speak of God as Father we may hesitate in case we read too much into the word. But our chief danger is in reading too little from it, drawing our ideas either from an earthly father's indulgence, caring too little for his children's training, or from his self-indulgence, taking the convenient path of a domestic tyrant.

Here, by contrast, we are made to see this title in terms of accepted cost and anguish. God as a father rebuffed, torn between agonizing alternatives, may seem too human altogether; but this is the price of bringing home to us the fact that divine love is more, not less, ardent and vulnerable than ours. 'For' (as verse 9 will remind us, correcting our inverted values) 'I am God, and not a man.' Once more, as in chapter 3, it is he, not we, who sets the pace and who stays the course against every discouragement and provocation that ingratitude can offer.

1. The cold shoulder (11:1–4)

More than once we have been reminded of the bright promise of Israel's youth, so rapidly to fade (see 6:4; 9:10; 10:1, 11; 13:1, 4–6). The promise arose out of God's grace rather than their good qualities, and the fading of it out of their sheer perversity – for it is one of Hosea's emphases that

Israel's sin, so far from springing from ignorance or hardship, was their reply to heaven's kindness and concern.

The grace of God shines out at once in the words *I loved him* (implying, when used by God, not the involuntary emotional reaction which it tends to mean to us, but a choice as free as it is affectionate),[1] and still more clearly in his naming Israel *my son.*

Incidentally, the quotation of this verse in Matthew 2:15 is far from arbitrary. Israel in its childhood was already set apart for the world's ultimate blessing, and was described to Pharaoh as God's 'firstborn son' (Exod. 4:22–23). By God's providence it had taken refuge in Egypt, but must return to its own land to fulfil its calling. Therefore, although it had been threatened with extinction through (among other things) the massacre of its infant sons, it was miraculously delivered. Not surprisingly the infant Christ, who summed up in his person all that Israel was called to be, was likewise threatened and delivered; and although the details differed, the early pattern was re-enacted in its essentials, ending with God's Son restored to God's land to fulfil the task marked out for him.

After that digression, the tragic anticlimax of verse 2 comes to us with added force. Between the great beginning and great fulfilment of the saying *I called my son*, there stretches the long age in which the words *I called*[2] received the worst of answers. There are similar sequences of *the more . . . the more*, equally perverse, at 4:7 and 10:1, and it would be a mistake to imagine that this off-handed reaction to divine love and to prosperity was confined to ancient Israel. Familiarity can still breed contempt, and success conceit, as though the very gifts that bring prosperity were not gifts at all, and the patient love of God were weakness.

The tenderness of verses 3 and 4 completes two (or perhaps one – see below) of the pictures God has used in nearby passages. Fatherly love, merely stated in verse 1, is now charmingly portrayed in a scene that any family will recognize, with the father absorbed in coaxing and supporting the child's first staggering steps; picking him up when he tires or tumbles; 'making the place better' when he hurts himself (though Isa. 66:13 will remind us that a father is only second-best at this). But Ephraim (that is,

---

[1] Note the 'not . . . because . . . But . . . because . . .' in Deut. 7:7–8, where God speaks more fully of this loving choice.

[2] 'The more I called . . .' etc. is the LXX reading, adopted (rightly, I think) by modern versions. The MT, with 'The more they called . . .' etc. makes the same point but leaves the 'they' (presumably the prophets) unintroduced and unidentified.

Israel) is a child no longer. Like some aloof and scornful adolescent, he has forgotten or never realized – or simply does not want to know – what he owes to this relationship.

The second picture, that of verse 4, seems to take up and surpass that of 10:11a (the contented heifer and the considerate master). The heavenly farmer is now shown, in retrospect, as having treated his beast more as a pet than as a working animal.[3] Every detail of this pampering drives home the extraordinary graciousness that Israel has experienced, far beyond anything that she had any right to expect, or any prospect of receiving at the hands of her new masters. The next paragraph will make the last point brutally clear.

2. The cruel consequences (11:5–7)

Ever since chapter 7, with its picture of Ephraim flitting between Egypt and Assyria like a flustered bird (7:11), every chapter has named one or both of these great powers as her obsession and her downfall. In the comment on 8:13 we saw something of the reproach and irony in the thought of a return to Egypt;[4] and now the word *return* is taken up and used most tellingly in both its senses, literal and spiritual. Nowhere is it plainer than here that the unseen movement of the soul in turning to God (5b; RSV 'refused to return to me') or turning away (7a) is the decisive one, to be followed by inevitable consequences in the realm that we call practical. The physical return to Egypt – as refugees! – was certain from the moment of their refusal of a spiritual return to God.

Likewise the rejection of God as king has to end not merely with the disappearance of the kings they chose instead of him (the theme of 10:3, 7, 15) but with the iron rule of a foreign superpower. If RSV is right in verse

---

[3] See RSV. An attractive alternative is to read verse 4 as continuing the metaphor of father and child, as in NIV (cf. GNB, JB, NEB, NRSV): *I led them with cords of human kindness, with ties of love. To them I was like one who lifts a little child to the cheek, and I bent down to feed them.* But this requires emending *'ōl* (yoke) to *'ûl* (baby, suckling), and *lĕḥêhem* (their cheeks or jaws) to *leḥyî* or *lĕḥāyay* (my cheek[s]) – and attractiveness is too little reason to alter a text that already makes sense. Admittedly the text seems disturbed elsewhere in the chapter (see on verse 7); but each passage must be treated on its own merits.

[4] As AV, RV indicate, the Heb. text has the word 'not' (*lō'*) before 'return'. But in view of the repeated predictions of such a return in 8:13; 9:3, 6; 11:11, NIV legitimately takes this as an implied question: *Will they not return . . . ?* (see the footnote to 4:16b, p. 44). An alternative is to follow LXX in reading this word as *lô* ('to him'), taken as the last word of verse 4 (e.g. JB: 'stooping down to him I gave him [*lô*] his food'), not the first word of verse 5. Sounding alike, *lō'* and *lô* were easily confused by copyists: cf. the famous example in Isa. 9:3a ('*not* increased the joy', AV, corrected by later translations to agree with 3b by reading *lô* rather than *lō'*). For a more subtle interpretation of our verse, distinguishing between a typical and a literal return to Egypt, see *The New Bible Commentary Revised* (IVP, 1970), *ad loc.*

7b (but it is rather a big 'if'), this 'yoke'[5] stands in marked contrast to the one that was handled so gently in verse 4; and on any reading of the text there is now held out no prospect of relief.

3. The warm resolve (11:8–9)

Suddenly the fearful mechanisms of moral cause and political effect, of national guilt and judgment, of betrayal and estrangement, are interrupted by this passionate intervention, purely from disinterested love. No matter that the Lord may now seem wholly swayed by impulse and emotion: we are nearer a true knowledge of him in such terms than in the bloodless definitions of theological philosophy. Elsewhere Scripture takes ample care of what such definitions seek to safeguard, but it never takes the warmth out of love, the fire out of anger or the audacity out of grace.

So the very thought of abandoning the people he has lived among (*among you*, 9) to an extinction like that of the cities of the plain[6] stirs God to strong revulsion. But how does this fit in with what in fact transpired? For Ephraim/Israel (the northern kingdom) fell in 722 BC and was deported to Assyria. One answer could be that she was given, after this prophecy, yet another chance to repent. More probably the answer lies in the remnant who threw in their lot with Judah, and whose descendants returned with them from Babylon (1 Chr. 9:1–3) to be part of the continuing Israel which meets us in the New Testament as the parent stock of the church (see Rom. 11). The next paragraph seems to bear this out.

4. The great homecoming (11:10–11)

God's mercy, in the great soliloquy of verses 8 and 9, decreed survival and a future for his people, when they deserved neither. But (as the rest of the book has shown) nothing facile would do, for without a change of heart survival would mean only a repetition of the past. So it is a chastened people, *trembling . . . trembling*, that will at last come home from being

---

[5] The Heb. text reads 'and (though) they call (upon) him to the height' (*'el 'al* – see footnote on 7:16), which NEB renders as 'though they call on their high god', while NIV interprets 'the height' (*'al*) as *God Most High* (cf. AV, NRSV). JB, however, treats *'al* as a miscopying of *ba'al* (Baal), and RSV revocalizes it as *'ōl*, 'yoke' (see footnote 3 above), and modifies the form and meaning of the verb 'to call', to yield the sentence 'they are appointed to the yoke'. This makes a striking companion to 10:11 and 11:4, but is excessively conjectural.

[6] Admah and Zeboyim were destroyed with Sodom and Gomorrah. Deut. 29:23 recalls this, in a passage which threatens Israel with just such a fate as theirs.

'wanderers among the nations' (9:17). The 'easily deceived and senseless' 'dove' of 7:11, always flitting between Egypt and Assyria, will have had its fill of both, and of the lands beyond the sea, and be thankful for its own nest. More important, it will be the Lord whom Israel will 'go after' (10, NRSV), not the 'lovers' whom she had once pursued (2:5).

All this is seen as happening only at his signal, the lion's roar with which he leaps into action – for the Bible consistently portrays the Day of the Lord as one of terror, by its judgment on a wicked world, though also of delight by its ending of that evil.[7]

It is not easy to know what stage of history is in mind here: whether some intermediate day of the lion's roar, such as the overthrow of Babylon which brought a remnant of Israel (including some from these northern tribes) home to Jerusalem (see again 1 Chr. 9:1–3); or the spiritual homecoming of God's *children* (10b) of many nations in the gospel age (in line with Paul's quotation of Hos. 2:23 and 1:10 in Rom. 9:25–26); or again the great turning of Israel to the Lord which is predicted in Romans 11:12, 25ff. What is certain is that the final event will far surpass our wisest thoughts and wildest expectations.

---

[7] While in Amos the lion's roar (Amos 1:2) announces an imminent series of local judgments, Jer. 25:30–38 presents it on a worldwide scale, and Joel 3:16 as enough to shake the universe. 'But', adds Joel, 'the Lord will be a refuge for his people.'

Hosea 11:12 [1] – 12:14

14. Look back and learn!

If we have any misgivings over treating the early stories of the Bible as texts for today, this chapter should dispel them. It reads almost as sermon notes on the life of Jacob and on the exodus from Egypt; and Hosea has already drawn on other potent incidents of the past as mirrors of the present and pointers to the future (e.g. 6:7 [?]; 9:9; 10:9f.; 11:1f.; cf. 13:10f.).

But first he is severely topical, assessing Ephraim and Judah as they are in his own day.

1. My Lord Time-server and my Lord Turn-about (11:12 – 12:2)

The heading we have given to this paragraph calls for two comments. First, the fanciful names come (as many readers will recognize) from Bunyan's *The Pilgrim's Progress*, where they sum up two leading citizens of the town of Fair-speech. But second, whereas Judah, to judge by the NIV text, deserves the second of these names, some translations would present him in a very different light. For example, NRSV:

> but Judah still walks with God,
>   and is faithful to the Holy One.

There are, however, two objections to NRSV's favourable picture. First, in the next breath God brings 'an indictment against Judah' (12:2, NRSV;

---

[1] In the Heb. Bible the new chapter begins at this earlier point, with good reason.

a charge ... against, NIV); and second, the statement that Judah still 'walks with God' and is faithful to him is based on the Septuagint, not the Hebrew text. The Hebrew says that Judah still 'plays fast and loose' with God.[2] The second line of that couplet must take this into account, as in, for example, NIV or NEB.[3]

So both kingdoms are rebuked, but chiefly Ephraim which is Hosea's mission field. One lesson that emerges from this pair of verses is that double-talk, whatever it does to the listener, certainly corrupts the talker. The religious *lies* and *deceit* of 11:12 are linked by more than chance with the inner emptiness and futile aims of 12:1a (another of Hosea's caustic little sketches) and with the double-dealing of 12:1b – for each reacts on the other. It happened this way in Hosea's time, in a downward spiral of meaningless religion (4:6; 7:14; 8:11ff.), moral anarchy (e.g. 4:1ff.), feverish hedonism (4:10ff.), perfidy in politics and diplomacy (7:6f., 11), and in the end, friendlessness (8:8–10) and ruin. It would not be hard to find at least parts of this pattern reproduced wherever other groups and nations have started on such a path.

Yet while the chapter takes us through some of these stages, it also braces us with reminders of what can happen when God and humans take hold of one another and when God's day of liberation dawns. So we turn our minds to a founding father and a formative event: to Jacob and to the exodus.

2. Wrestling Jacob (12:3–6)

In only a stroke or two the first couplet brings the whole of Jacob's story into focus by means of his two names, Jacob and Israel. The glimpse of him, born with his hand clutching Esau's heel (Gen. 25:26), gave him his birth name ('he-is-at-the-heel');[4] and for years his dealings with his fellows were to confirm all that was sinister in the name, as of one who steals up from behind to outwit and overreach you. Esau, who was

---

[2] The Heb. *rād* is from the root *rwd*, the verb used in Jer. 2:31 to express playing truant, running wild ('we have broken away', NEB; 'we are free', NRSV). And AV, RV had to emend *rād* to *rādâ* to arrive at their translation, 'ruleth'.

[3] NIV (*even against the faithful Holy One*) sounds a little forced, but cf. GNB, RV mg. Alternatively NEB may be right in interpreting the plural word *qĕdôšîm* not as 'the Holy One', but in its more obvious sense as 'holy ones'; hence, freely, 'still loyal to the idols he counts holy'.

[4] Normally the name, which is found elsewhere in the ancient world, would mean 'May He (God) be at your heels', i.e. be your rearguard. But, like the name Isaac ('May He smile' [upon you]), it had a double meaning within the family, commemorating a very special moment.

bargained out of his birthright and tricked out of his blessing, cried, 'Isn't he rightly named Jacob? This is the second time he has taken advantage of me ['Jacobed me']' (Gen. 27:36). Even Laban, that master of manoeuvre, found he had met his match in this man.

His ultimate name, Israel, speaks very differently: of tenacity without stealth ('he strives'), and of a preoccupation, in the last resort, not with a man but with God.[5] The transformation that this implies is put with beautiful economy in the first two lines of verse 4, initially portraying his aggression and will to win, redirected now towards the nobler end of having power with God (yet still in terms of imposing his own will on his great adversary), but finally portraying him as a suppliant for grace; his arrogance broken, but not his eagerness. The story is told in Genesis 32:22–32.

Even so, verse 4 has one more point to make: that the remaking of the man had its origin not in his own enterprise, but in God's initiative revealed at Bethel long before (Gen. 28:10–22), in that classic display of grace unexpected, unsought and overwhelming.

Hosea is about to drive the lesson home with the great appeal of verse 6: 'But *you* . . .' But before he does so he reiterates the name of God, dwelling on it in verse 5 with special emphasis. If we wonder why he pauses at this point, we may notice that, for once, he has called the chief shrine of northern Israel by its right name, Bethel, 'house of God', instead of by its savage nickname Beth Aven, 'house of wickedness'. For it was *God* whom Jacob had met there: God, not a golden calf (10:5; 13:2); and if Israel would learn from Jacob, this was the first lesson it must face.

Now, in verse 6, the heartfelt challenge can be made: *But you must return* – for your name is not Jacob/Israel for nothing! If you are more 'Jacob' than 'Israel', so was he when the call came, in the far country, with the words, 'Go back to the land of your fathers . . . and I will be with you.'[6] And if he received his new name when he insisted 'I will not let you go unless you bless me', so you are to be equally in earnest: to 'hold fast' (NRSV) to his will, and *wait . . . always* for his presence. (This is all the more pointed on account of its background in 6:1–6, where Israel's love was 'like the early dew that disappears'.)

---

[5] Israel appears to mean basically 'May God strive (for him)', but the wrestling context gave it the force of 'He strives with God' (Gen. 32:28).

[6] Gen. 31:3; cf. 35:1, '. . . to Bethel . . . to God, who appeared to you when you were fleeing from your brother Esau.'

If this seems too high a challenge, we overlook Hosea's nuance in phrasing it not simply as 'Return to', but rather, 'by the help of your God[7] return'. Nothing is then impossible.

3. Affluent Ephraim (12:7–9)

Anticlimax! Ephraim's is no wistful refusal like the rich young ruler's, but brazen, Laodicean (cf. Rev. 3:17) – and worse still, Canaanite. For 'Canaan' is the word translated here *The merchant*, branding Ephraim a true successor to the old corrupt inhabitants of the land. In cold print, his bland assurance that his extorted riches carry no guilt – or none to speak of[8] – and even put him above the law is patently absurd. Yet human attitudes, which venerate success and, at a safe distance, admire a clever rogue, still help to build up this cocksureness in people who sell their souls to the present.

To this, God's answer is another flashback to the past – this time not Jacob but the exodus. He makes his point first from the opening salvo of the Ten Commandments, *I have been the LORD your God ever since you came out of Egypt* – words as familiar to them as the Lord's Prayer is to us – and then from the ritual of the pilgrim feast of tabernacles.

It is a double thrust. First (in effect): 'Was it for *this* that I redeemed you? To make you a bunch of Canaanites?' And second: 'When you relive the exodus each year, camping out as your ancestors did, is it only make-believe? Or is it to relearn the lesson of those days, that man does not live on bread alone?'

So, if they will only take it, there is healing and not mere doom in God's resolve to strip away the comforts that have turned these pilgrims into profiteers. The apparent threat, *I will make you live in tents again* (9), is of a piece with what was said in 2:14–15:

> Therefore I am now going to allure her;
> > I will lead her into the wilderness
> > and speak tenderly to her . . .

---

[7] So RSV, NEB; cf. this Heb. preposition in, e.g., 1:7 (RSV): 'I will deliver them *by* the LORD . . . not *by* bow, nor *by* sword', etc.; likewise the well-known Zech. 4:6. Alternatively it may imply 'return (and rest) *in* thy God' (so BDB, p. 88b).

[8] The Hebrew of 8b (9b, Heb.) is most accurately rendered in RV: 'they shall find in me none iniquity that were sin.'

There she will respond as in the days of her youth,
> as in the day she came up out of Egypt.

This is the spirit of the whole book. But just because it seeks a free response, it may be met with obdurate refusal; and there is no attempt to hide that possibility or to mask its fatal consequences.

4. Prophets without honour (12:10–14)

The close of the chapter has the broken, disjointed sound of agitation and distress. But the way verse 13 reverts to the opening theme (10), the role of *the prophets*, suggests that here at least there is a unifying thread, a central emphasis. It is that God's dealings with human beings have always been directed to the mind and conscience, which are the prophets' great concern; and the nation will be judged on that high plane alone.

The opening verse (10) goes out of its way to stress the fact that God, not a man, is the fount and origin of prophecy (*I spoke . . .*) and of its strange and varied ways of speaking. 'The prophet is . . . a fool,' people were saying; 'the inspired person a maniac' (9:7); but the prophet's visions and parables were not mere eccentricities: they were the word of God. This at once raises the question (for us as much as for the ancient Israelites) why God, who could speak with the precision of a lawgiver and the persuasive clarity of a wisdom teacher, should also dazzle us with visions and tease us with parables. The answer, at least in part, is that the prophet was sent to make people *think*, and to confront them with the signs of their own time and with the living God, who is not shut away timelessly behind his laws and liturgies, but turns upon us 'his glorious presence' (as Isaiah puts it: Isa. 3:8) and brings whole nations into judgment.

So – and here is the connection between verses 10 and 11 – God names actual places, far and near, that are ripening for judgment, and pours fine scorn on pious superstitions, punning on the falsely venerated Gilgal with the disrespectful plural of *gal*, 'a rubble heap'. This divine impatience with religiosity burned fiercely in the prophets, especially in Hosea's great contemporaries, Amos, Micah and Isaiah, but supremely in our Lord, whose sustained invective in Matthew 23 surpasses even that of the Old Testament for both brilliance of expression and depth of concern.

Passing over verse 12 for the moment, verse 13's repetition, *a prophet ... by a prophet*, makes a more important point than may appear at first sight. It is not simply that the prophets can trace their spiritual lineage back to Moses, though this is true.[9] Rather, it insists that the exodus was above all a spiritual event, not just a liberation movement. Moses' greatness was not that he stood up to Pharaoh, but that he stood before God and knew him face to face. Mount Sinai, first with the revelation at the burning bush, and subsequently with the giving of the law and covenant, gave the whole enterprise its point. It was no mere detour, no formal church parade on the march to victory. 'I carried you on eagles' wings and brought you *to myself.*'[10] Here, in knowing God, was Israel's *raison d'être* and true stability: *by a prophet he cared for him* – for 'where there is no revelation, people cast off restraint' (Prov. 29:18).

It is still more fatal, as the final verse makes clear, to have prophecy and no use for it. That was how Ephraim aroused God's *bitter anger*. It is the special danger of a once-enlightened nation, church or individual, whose appetite for truth has failed for lack of exercise in what John would call '*doing* truth' (cf. John 3:21, AV).

5. Additional note on Hosea 12:12

Verse 12 seems to be a parenthesis, supplying the missing part of the patriarch's life story as summarized in verse 3, where it was perhaps excluded so as to leave the Jacob–Israel contrast all the clearer. But its present place may have a subtler purpose. J. L. Mays draws attention to the repetition of the Hebrew root for 'tended' (*tended ... cared for*) in verses 12 and 13 (13–14, Heb.), and sees in this an implied contrast between the human shepherd, so limited in scope, and the divine one – for it could well be that Israel found its pride and reassurance too much in its former ancestor, too little in the living God of the exodus and the prophets. That ancestor is therefore portrayed now in the soberest of colours: a fugitive rather than a pilgrim, a keeper of sheep rather than the shepherd of a nation; his motivation, for years, totally domestic. Hero worship, we are gently reminded, is seldom even true to the past, let alone valid for the present.

---

[9] See Deut. 18:15–22, which foresees a line of prophets between Moses and the ultimate prophet, Christ (cf. Acts 3:22ff.).

[10] Exod. 19:4, spoken at Mount Sinai. Cf. Exod. 3:12, 18.

Hosea 13:1–16

15. The unmaking of a kingdom

This is the climax of Hosea's prophecies of doom, but not the climax of the book. That distinction is reserved (apart from one remarkable verse here) for the next chapter, the great vision of renewal; but both were due to be fulfilled. The northern kingdom, as we have already seen, was due to fall in 722 BC, never to reappear; but the New Testament already celebrates the greater things that were to lie beyond this tragedy.

The one dazzling exception (as I see it) to the darkness of this chapter is the great taunt of verse 14 against the last enemy. Most modern translations, unhappily, turn this upside down, in the supposed interests of consistency; the NIV gives a more literal rendering.

1. Vanished dignity (13:1–3)

If there is one fact about human fortunes which history almost dins into us, it is their instability; and historians can show any number of economic, political and other reasons for the changes that turn the giants of one era into the weaklings of the next. Here, neither the power changes abroad nor the factions at home are blamed for the sad state of Ephraim, but a much earlier and subtler shift within the mind: from the Lord to Baal. At that point Ephraim *died*, as surely as Adam did, although like Adam he went on living, to all outward appearances. To make it still more imperceptible, this fickleness had posed as only a broadening of the way in which one served the Lord, as the comments on chapter 2 have shown. But such pluralism ignored the very first commandment (pointedly alluded to in verse 4 and previously in 12:9), and led straight on, by its veneration of idols, to the breaking of the second. There is a powerful jolt administered in verse 2 by the sudden change of focus, from the spectacle of skilful craftsmen and precious metals to that of the religious idiocy they served. The end of the expensive exercise, one which employed the talents of God's highest creatures, is presented in three scandalized words: *They* ['humans', *'ādām*] *kiss calf-idols!*

Earlier in the book (6:4) God had likened the goodness of Ephraim and Judah to *the morning mist* and to the short-lived dew of dawn.[1] Now he presses the point right home – for a nation *is* no more than its morals and its character. So not only their shallow resolves, but *they* themselves, will simply vanish from the scene. What is said of them is said elsewhere of individual sinners (*like chaff*, Ps. 1:4) and of all enemies of God (*like smoke*, Ps. 68:2).

2. No tame divinity (13:4–8)

Nothing could be further than the two halves of this paragraph from the popular picture of God as a tolerant spectator. First he insists on fully personal relations (*You shall acknowledge*[2] . . . ; *I cared for you*) and on exclusive loyalty; then, for the breach of this, threatens to turn from saviour (4) into predator. In terms of the Ten Commandments, whose opening declaration seems to underlie these verses (4a), he is 'a jealous God'; and these threats of carnage make no apologies for the fact.

It need hardly be said that the childishness that makes up most of human jealousy has no place in God: only a fiery concern for what is precious to him. It is as far from our 'envy, hatred and malice' as it is from cool indifference. Equally, there is nothing arbitrary in his judgments, excessive though they will often seem to us, and as uninhibited as in the ferocious picture of verse 8. The rest of the book must be allowed to put to us the other side of it, showing us not only the logic of our spiritual sowing and reaping (e.g. 8:7, 'the wind . . . the whirlwind'; 10:13, 'the fruit of deception'), our deafness to reason and appeal (8:12; 11:2), our obstinacy (4:16; 11:7), evasiveness (7:13) and wantonness (5:4), but supremely the deep reluctance of God to resort to judgment (11:8), and

---

[1] The Heb. of 6:4b is exactly echoed in our verse 3a.

[2] NRSV's present tense, 'you know . . .', is not the most obvious translation, and it breaks the implied link with the first commandment, whose statement *I have been the* LORD leads to the series of demands (*you shall* . . .) which are all expressed in the Heb. tense that we have here. AV, RV, NIV rightly translate it as a future.

his longing that at last it may bring his people to their senses (5:13–15; chapter 14).

3. Who can help you? (13:9–13)

The mood in which Israel had demanded a king is quite familiar to us: a compound of reasonable grievances (against misrule by Samuel's sons, 1 Sam. 8:1–5), ideas of grandeur ('such as all the other nations have') and trust in the seen rather than the unseen ('a king . . . to go out before us and fight our battles', 1 Sam. 8:20).

Yet God made room for kingship and put it to noble use, as he still does with our bright ideas – or in spite of them. What he could not bless was the arrogance that gave rise to it and the power struggles that exploited it. We have already seen its corruption in Hosea's day (7:3–7), and the utter disillusion that marked its downfall (10:3: 'But even if we had a king, what could he do for us?'). The process by which God *in* [his] *wrath . . . took* [these kings] *away* was of their own choosing: a string of assassinations and coups from within, and the punitive might of Assyria from without, in reprisal for repeated acts of treachery.[3]

Hosea's wealth of imagery, perhaps unequalled among the prophets, is drawn on once again in verses 12 and 13 for a double thrust at Israelite complacency: first by picturing unforgiven sin as a well-kept store of trouble for the future, and then by the analogy of a birth that threatens to go fatally wrong. This second picture combines the tantalizing thought of early promise that has come to nothing with that of a disaster that no-one can now avert. King Hezekiah of Judah would one day use this very metaphor, not in blank despair but in desperate appeal to God, and be answered by a miracle (2 Kgs 19:3ff.). In the northern kingdom there was no leader of that calibre or that faith.

4. The last enemy (13:14)

Is this a ringing challenge to 'the last enemy', signalling his doom, or is it (as some would urge) nothing but the last nail in Israel's coffin? The NIV translation, agreeing with the New Testament (1 Cor. 15:54–55) and with the older versions as far back as the pre-Christian LXX, takes it as a great

---

[3] 2 Kgs 15:8 – 17:6. See also the last six names of kings of Israel, and what befell them, on p. 109.

affirmation, one of the greatest in Scripture. That is, it treats the opening couplet of this verse as a straight promise, exactly as it is written; a promise to be unfolded by our Lord's great 'ransom' saying in Mark 10:45. Sadly, the modern trend is to turn it into a question expecting the answer 'No', and thereby to make the rest of the verse merely a call for the weapons of death to do their worst against Israel.[4]

So it needs to be pointed out that the Hebrew of 14a does *not* use the interrogative prefix, but has the form of a plain statement. Sometimes, to be sure, the context of a verse compels us to read a statement ironically or with an interrogative inflexion (see the footnote on 4:16b), and this is why the present verse has suffered this treatment in some recent versions, for the surrounding gloom is certainly profound.

But what has been forgotten is that one of the outstanding features of this book is its sudden changes of tone from the sternest of threats to the warmest of resolves – most famously in 11:8:

> How can I give you up, Ephraim?
> How can I hand you over, Israel? . . .
> My heart is changed within me . . .

or in, for example, 1:9–10: 'Then the LORD said, "Call him Lo-Ammi (which means 'not my people') . . . Yet . . . they will be called 'children of the living God'."' Indeed the overall structure of the prophecy leads through judgment into the 'broad, sunlit uplands' of the final chapter, just as in fact the disastrous history of Israel and Judah turned out to be the prelude to the very destruction of death that is promised here.[5] The *compassion* God withholds in the final line is, of course, withheld not from the victims of death and the grave, but from this pair of tyrants themselves. Compare the personifying of them in Revelation 20:14: 'Then death and Hades were thrown into the lake of fire.' In less pictorial terms, God promises the utter end of death and its dominion, with no question of his modifying that resolve.[6]

---

[4] This is the point of NRSV, JB, made doubly explicit in NEB: 'Oh, for your plagues, O death!' (etc.), and in GNB, 'Bring on your plagues, death!' (etc.).

[5] A further detail in 14b, confirming the nature of the verse as a taunt against the last enemy, is that our Heb. text has 'I will be ['*hy*] your plagues, O death; I will be ['*hy*] your destruction, O Sheol.' LXX evidently used a text which had '*yh* ('Where?') at the points where MT has '*hy* ('I will be'). The difference becomes a major one only when the text is reinterpreted with NRSV, NEB, etc.

[6] Another interpretation of this final line, however, is that it introduces the next oracle (15–16), as NIV suggests by its spacing and punctuation.

5. No quarter for Samaria (13:15–16)

The name Ephraim had the attractive sound of *thrives* or 'flourishing' (15a), and had been chosen for that reason: 'It is because God', said Joseph, 'has made me fruitful in the land of my suffering' (Gen. 41:52). In comparison with Judah and some of her southern cousins,[7] the northern kingdom of Ephraim/Israel was fertile, and had recently been very prosperous. But, in common with all material prosperity, Ephraim's wealth was as vulnerable to an aggressor as an orchard to an east wind.

And what an aggressor! Assyria was noted for its cruelty in war, and would certainly not stop short of the atrocities which lesser powers allowed themselves. There is a sickening frequency of references to the butchery described in 16b: see the list in the footnote to 10:14b.

So the prophet refuses to soften his warning by clothing it in abstract terms. The fate that his people were bringing on themselves would be all too sharp and physical, pressed home in revolting detail. But mercifully, although it would mean the end of all that they had promised themselves, it was not the last word from God.

---

7 The Heb. text of 15a has 'flourish among brothers', which hardly needs the emendation to 'among rushes' as in NRSV.

Hosea 14:1–9

16. The way home

This little chapter of only nine verses,[1] as quiet and gentle as its predecessors were tumultuous, leads us back again through the main areas of the book, this time on our way home. Israel is being beckoned, and the way is signposted with the landmarks she passed on her spiritual journey into the far country.

1. Draw near to God . . . (14:1–3)

The first word, *Return*, is an old friend, a strong feature of the book. Up to now it has brought only disappointment and reproach. Basically it means 'turn'; and Israel has habitually turned the wrong way. They have been 'determined to turn from me', as 11:7 puts it. This, incidentally, was obscured by the older translations that spoke of 'backsliding', which has a sound of failure rather than perversity, whereas in fact there had been a flat refusal to respond (11:5), born of pride (7:10) and of settled preference ('Their deeds do not permit them to return to their God', 5:4). Any response to the great call 'Come, let us return to the LORD' had so far been as shallow as a passing impulse (6:1, 4).

But God will not give up – how could he (cf. 11:8–9)? If their repentance has been shallow, he will deepen it. There is warmth in the emphatic form of the word *return* here (1a; verse 2 uses the ordinary form), and the preposition is a strong one.[2] We could almost translate it, 'Oh turn, Israel,

---

[1] The Heb. Bible has ten verses, through starting the chapter at 13:16; so its numbering runs one verse ahead of the English versions throughout the chapter.

[2] Cf. BDB, p. 724a, citing this verse (14:2, Heb.).

right back to the Lord.' Even the familiar words *your God* have gained a new intensity from the threat which Israel's fickleness had seemed to pose to her marriage bond with the Lord. Against all deserving, the marriage holds; he is still hers. Here is the costly equivalent of his word to the cuckolded Hosea: 'Go, show your love to your wife again, though she is loved by another man and is an adulteress. Love her as the LORD loves the Israelites, though they turn to other gods' (3:1).

Repentance, then, will have to start with the matter of the broken loyalty. 'I am now going to allure her . . . and . . . she will respond as in the days of her youth' (2:14–15). As George Adam Smith finely puts it, 'Amos cries, "Turn, for in front of you is destruction"; but Hosea, "Turn, for behind you is God."'[3]

For all its warmth, though, God's calling is exacting. It leaves no room for humbug: there must be 'fruit in keeping with repentance'. Already 12:6 has held up to us the challenging implications of this. Towards our fellow human beings it will mean 'Maintain love and justice'; and towards heaven, 'Wait for your God always.' It is the second of these that our chapter will be chiefly spelling out.

First, then, *Take* words *with you* (2). Words can be facile, but so can actions. A major contrast in this book is between articulate, meaningful encounter and the mere formalities and offerings which people try to substitute for it. 'When they go with their flocks and herds to seek the LORD, they will not find him' (5:6). Sub-personal religion never will (cf. 5:15).

These *words* are to be without reservations or excuses. God has spoken of *your sins* (1); his people must accept and echo that (2), not jib at it or play it down as they did in 12:8 with their boast, 'they will not find in me any iniquity or sin.'

But what of the next plea, translated in NRSV as 'accept that which is good'? The AV and the NIV, perhaps scenting salvation by works, gave the rather forced translation *receive us graciously*. G. A. F. Knight mentions another just-possible rendering, 'Receive (us), O Good One.' But more probably it is simply a plea that God will accept the offering from the lips and the heart which he has required of his people. This chimes in with the famous saying in 6:6 about the things he desires above sacrifice, and with Psalm 51:17; perhaps, too, with the verbal echo, obscured in

---

[3] Smith, p. 339.

translation, between God's call, 'Take ... with you', and our response, 'Accept [lit. 'take'] ...'

The offering of words, which began with one kind of confession, the acknowledgment of sin, now turns into confession in its other sense, the acknowledgment of God in praise. The Hebrew of verse 2c is awkward again: literally, 'and we will render bullocks, our lips'; but at least the word 'render' gives a good clue to the sense. It is the term used for paying one's vows (e.g. Ps. 116:14) in due gratitude for answered prayer. Lips, then, will be our votive offering, our sacrificial 'bullocks'. But the point is made more gracefully in the Greek and Syriac versions, which read the same consonants to mean *the fruit of our lips*, and this is how Hebrews 13:15 quotes it.

So far, then, the positive side of repentance has been uppermost. The runaways must return, the sinners plead, the formalists use their minds and lips, to come back into fellowship with God. It is a turning to the light.

Now with verse 3 comes the negative requirement, a turning *from* the old ways, in a clear farewell to futile hopes and false beliefs. Both are familiar from the earlier chapters. For security, Israel has been playing a double game, banking on Assyria at one moment, and on Egypt (that source of horses and chariots, 3a; cf. Isa. 31:1) the next. We have seen those two names in almost every chapter since the middle of the book – for Israel was as loth as we are to play these matters straight, or to take God seriously. *His* name carried no weight in politics.

As for false beliefs, the gods of verse 3b are constantly in evidence throughout the book. Hosea's scorn for them is as total as Israel's infatuation. No doubt our own scorn echoes his. But as long as *what our own hands have made* looms larger to us than the One who made these hands, verse 3b will still have words for us to use.

The trustful climax of the confession is beautifully, if freely, expressed in NEB: 'for in thee the fatherless finds a father's love' – which brings out the allusion in the Hebrew to the way the book began, with the prophet's broken marriage and disowned daughter, Lo-Ruhamah, which means virtually 'Unloved' (1:6). For Lo-Ruhamah was to be renamed Ruhamah, 'She is loved' (2:1, 23),[4] in token of the Lord's reclaiming grace for Israel. Once

---

[4] The verb which NRSV translates here in terms of 'mercy', and in chapters 1 and 2 in terms of 'pity', is translated 'love' in NIV (see Ps. 18:1 [2, Heb.]).

again this chapter has taken up the opening themes of the book, filling them with hope.

2. . . . and he will draw near to you (14:4–7)

Now God speaks, and the whole scene lights up before us. The word '(Re)turn' still echoes through the chapter, as it has echoed through the whole book. It was heard in verses 1 and 2, and will reappear in verse 7; meanwhile it comes twice in verse 4, first concealed in the word *waywardness* (lit. 'turning'; i.e. 'apostasy', NEB), to remind us that our waywardness is incurable until God heals it; and then in the assurance of the last line that his anger has *turned* away. Between these two reminders of the past comes one of the purest expressions of what the New Testament will call grace, prevailing over the language of judgment and desert heard in 9:15 ('I will no longer love them'). The NEB translates our present line, 'Of my own bounty will I love them.' We can notice, too, a telling contrast, not only between this outgoing love and the scant affection of Israel's paramours (2:7), but between this tireless Giver and the reluctant hirelings of 8:8–9.

After the perfect clarity of these promises – and clarity is vital to the anxious and conscience-stricken – the poetry is free to spread itself in the next verses (5–7). All the imagery of them is from nature, at its happiest and most bountiful.

Without labouring the details, we can gain from this a threefold impression of Israel revived and reconciled to God. First, freshness (dew, flowers, fragrance, beauty, shade); second, stability (rooted like the poplar, perhaps; or like Lebanon, 5);[5] third, vigour (the spreading shoots of new growth, 6; the 'corn in abundance', 7, NEB).[6]

But such a summary is useful only if it makes us look more closely at the passage, which has all the grace and vitality to match the realities of which it speaks. There is nothing stifling or constricting in the divine love expressed here. Like the river of Ezekiel 47, it brings life to everything it reaches.

---

[5] Many modern versions reckon that *Lebanon*, the final word of each of the next two verses (6 and 7, or in the Heb. Bible 7 and 8), has induced a scribal error in verse 5, where they conjecture that *libnê* (poplar) stood originally. But the Heb. text is supported by the ancient versions in ending all three verses with *Lebanon*, which is not only poetically effective but, in verse 5, is perfectly intelligible, as referring either to its mountain range or (NIV) to its cedars.

[6] See NRSV mg. The Heb. text has 'they shall make corn [*dāgān*] flourish' (lit. 'live'), which NIV has emended to *they will flourish like the corn* (*gan*).

3. The appeal pressed home (14:8)

Ephraim! Such an exclamation has more than once already laid bare
the heart of the prophecy and of its ultimate Author. Like David's cry,
'O Absalom, my son, my son!' (2 Sam. 18:33), or our Lord's 'Jerusalem, Jerusalem' (Matt. 23:37), it has voiced both love and anguish: 'What can I do
with you, Ephraim?' 'How can I give you up, Ephraim?' (6:4; 11:8). Now (as
I see it) it is as though God turns to reason with the hearer for the last
time – for the penitent words of verses 2 and 3 and the fair prospect of
verses 4–7 were part of an invitation (1–2a) which has yet to be accepted
and made Israel's own.

The plea (on this view)[7] rests on the incomparable claims of God. Can
he any longer[8] be spoken of, even thought of, in the same breath as idols?
Can Egypt's or Assyria's protection compete with his? Do they answer
when you call? Do they care as he cares?

The last two lines of this verse read strangely until we remember that
Hebrew thought has none of our inhibitions against mixed metaphors.
God, these lines can well be saying, has all the constancy of the evergreen
(cf. NRSV), all the richness of the fruit tree. Ephraim, if he is to live up to
his own name ('God has made me fruitful', Gen. 41:52), need look no
further.

4. Epilogue: to the reader . . . (14:9)

Whether the prophet himself or an editor added these words need hardly
concern us here. The point they drive home is that the prophecy is open-
ended: its eloquence and passion could win Israel to repentance or could
leave her unmoved. The response was hers to make.

But not only hers. The *Who* of this verse suddenly exposes us to the
same searching encounter, for the word of God goes on speaking; it never
slips safely into the past. The rightness of God's ways as revealed in this
book is so far above us in both holiness and love as to leave self-sufficient

---

[7] The English versions reflect something of the variety of possible interpretations. In the first line, JB,
GNB and NEB ('What has Ephraim to do with idols any more?') make use of LXX. In AV, RV, Ephraim is the speaker.
In the last two lines, opinions differ as to the identity of the speaker or speakers; it has even been suggested
that in the four lines of the verse, God and Ephraim speak alternately (Pusey).

[8] NIV eases the question by omitting 'any longer'. But the note of time is intelligible if it refers to the
effect of the prophecy on the hearers' understanding.

human beings without excuse, self-condemned, while those who turn into the way of righteousness find themselves met more than halfway.

> To turn aside from thee is hell,
>> To walk with thee is heaven.[9]

The comment of G. A. F. Knight on this verse deserves to be the last word:

> Therefore, dear reader, so runs the content of this Epilogue, ask yourself the question – how would you apply this message of Hosea to your own knowledge and experience of Israel's God?

---

[9] J. G. Whittier, 'Immortal Love, for Ever Full'.

Addenda

Maps
Chronological table
A bird's-eye view of the book

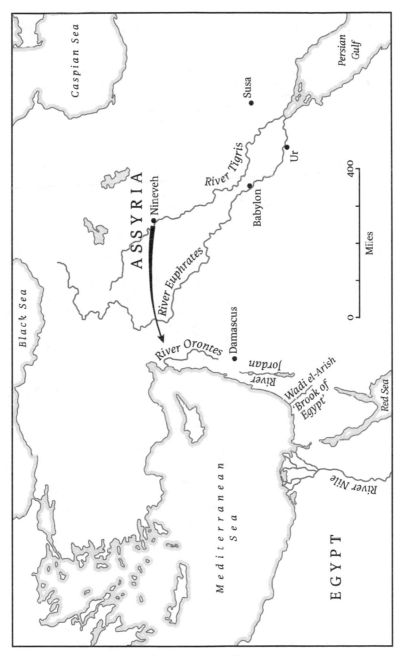

Assyria and the West

Between 734 and 722 BC the kingdom of Israel and most of its northern neighbours were reduced to petty provinces of the Assyrian Empire.

In 734/3, Galilee, Gilead and the coastal strip were taken (2 Kgs 15:29; Isa. 9:1), to become the provinces of Megiddo, Gilead and Dor.

Finally, in 724–722, Samaria was besieged and taken, and its king replaced by an imperial governor. The new provinces were populated, to be resettled with peoples from distant parts of the empire (2 Kgs 17:24–41).

Riblah
Assyrian Province of Hamath

Byblos

SIDONIANS

Assyrian Province of Subite

Assyrian Province of Mansuate

Sidon

Damascus

Assyrian Province of Damascus

Tyre

Dan

Mediterranean Sea

FIRST PARTS LOST BY ISRAEL 734/3

Arbela

Assyrian Province of Karnaim

Dor

Megiddo
Jezreel

(Arbela?)

Assyrian Province of Hauran

Assyrian Province of Dor

Samaria

Assyrian Province of Gilead

RUMP OF ISRAEL 734/3–722

River Jordan

Adam

Joppa

Bethel

AMMON

Ashdod

Gilgal

Ashkelon

Jerusalem

Gaza

PHILISTINES

Dead Sea

JUDAH

MOAB

Beersheba

Wadi el-Arish

0   40

Miles

EDOM

The break-up of Israel

The kingdoms of Judah (the south) and Israel (the north) from the death of Solomon to the fall of Samaria

Kings of Judah	(Prophets)	Kings of Israel
931 Rehoboam		931 Jeroboam I
913 Abijam		
911 Asa		910 Nadab, killed by
		↙
		909 Baasha
		886 Elah, killed by
		↙
		885 Zimri: suicide, on defeat by
		↙
		885 Omri
870 Jehoshaphat (father's co-regent from 873) (see footnote on co-regency p. 111)	(Elijah)	874 Ahab
		853 Ahaziah
848 Jehoram (father's co-regent from 853)	(Elisha)	852 Jehoram, killed by ↙
841 Ahaziah, killed by ⟶		841 Jehu
841 Queen Athaliah		

Assyrian aggression against Israel and her neighbours

Kings of Assyria

Assyrian campaigns reach Lebanon and the coast of Philistia, terrorizing and extorting tribute.	Ashur-nasir-pal II 883–859
853 Westward drive halted at the battle of Qarqar, by a coalition headed by Syria and Israel. King Ahab supplied 2,000 chariots and 14,000 men, according to the Assyrian records.	Shalmaneser III 859–824
841 Assyrians besiege Damascus and its king Hazael, then storm round Palestine, exacting tribute from (among others) King Jehu of Israel.	Shalmaneser III 859–824

Kings of Judah	(Prophets)	Kings of Israel
835 Joash		
		814 Jehoahaz
796 Amaziah		798 Joash
767 Uzziah (Azariah) (father's co-regent from 791)	(Jonah)	782 Jeroboam II (father's co-regent from 793)
	(Amos) (Hosea)	
		753 Zechariah, killed by ↙
		752 Shallum, killed by ↙
		752 Menahem
		742 Pekahiah, killed by ↙
740 Jotham (father's co-regent from 750)	(Isaiah) (Micah)	740 Pekah, killed by
732 Ahaz (father's co-regent from 744)		732 Hoshea

| 804–802 | Assyria crushes Damascus. Israel, long harassed by Hazael of Damascus, now enters a half-century of peace and affluence. | Adad-nirari III 810–781 |

Tiglath-pileser III, 745–727

| 734–732 | Menahem had reigned as Tiglath-pileser's vassal, but c. 735 King Pekah conspires with Damascus, Gaza, etc., against Assyria. Assyria sweeps down the Philistine coast, truncates Israel (see map) and takes Damascus. But Hoshea assassinates Pekah and submits to Assyria to preserve what is left of Israel. | Tiglath-pileser III, 745–727 |

Kings of Judah	Kings of Israel
	722 THE FALL OF SAMARIA (the end of the northern kingdom)
715 Hezekiah (father's co-regent from 729)	

---

[1] The practice of co-regency (evidenced by the overlapping dates of certain kings) was presumably a precaution against disputes over the succession, as well as a means of giving the crown prince experience of government. Note Judah's stable dynasty, the house of David, in contrast to Israel's many coups and changes.

724–
722

Hoshea now plots with Egypt against Assyria. Shalmaneser has him seized, and invades Israel. The capital, Samaria, holds out from 724 to 722, then falls to Sargon II, Shalmaneser's successor. Israel's inhabitants are deported, to be replaced by other subject peoples.

Shalmaneser V
727–722

Sargon II
722–705

A bird's-eye view of the book

Part 1: A parable from life
A DISTRACTED FAMILY
(Hosea 1 – 3)

1:1 – Introducing Hosea

1:2–9 – An ominous beginning

At God's command, Hosea takes a wife who, he knows, will be unfaithful to him, just as Israel has been unfaithful to the Lord. This woman bears three children and then leaves him. Each child is given a name that is eloquent of God's displeasure with his people and of their impending judgment.

1:10 – 2:1 – A rift in the clouds

The ominous names are not God's last word. At once, as though he cannot bear to leave the matter there, he points to the far future, when everything that these names have stood for will be reversed.

2:2–23 – The lovers and the Lover

Now it is the runaway mother (Israel, seen as God's unfaithful wife) who is the subject. She has left me, says God, for what her lovers promised her: all the fertile wealth of nature. She little knew that I myself, not her new gods, was the giver of it all!

So I will stop the flow, until she has nothing left but shame. Then I will court her again, and at last she will respond. This time it will be for ever. It will be like paradise regained; and the whole family will be at one.

3:1–5 – 'Love . . . as the Lord loves'

Now Hosea is sent to win back his own fickle wife, with love like the Lord's love. He has to buy her back – such is her new friend. Then he makes it clear that, from now on, no-one must come between them.

So too, after the discipline of long privation, a chastened Israel will at last come truly home.

Part 2: The parable spelt out
HOW CAN I GIVE YOU UP?
(Hosea 4 – 14)

4:1–19 – A people without understanding

Israel! You are a moral jungle! I charge you with every sin in the book. But you, sir priest, are the true villain. You, the teacher, have no use for knowledge, when knowledge could have saved my people. So I have no use for you. You and your flock will take your punishment together.

Can this be my people? Pagan and promiscuous, stubborn and sodden, you are fit for neither humankind nor God: only to be left to your own devices.

5:1–14 – The prospect darkens

Priests, people, king! I find you as treacherous as a trap, as tainted as a prostitute. You may think that you can choose your moment to repent, and can buy your way back into favour. But your sins are too strong for you, and your God has withdrawn.

Yes, I myself will hasten your decay, and I am now your predator; so no power on earth can help you.

You must learn the hard way now.

5:15 – 7:2 – Let us press on to know the Lord

When I am hard on you, and hard to find, it is to get you seeking. I must have your loyal love, not your fleeting piety or your sacrifices.

But what do I find? Nothing but disloyalty, nothing but violence, and not a flicker of concern.

7:3–16 – Decadence

Will the king and court, guardians of justice, stem this tide of evil? But they wallow and revel in it, and their revelry is murderous.

The whole nation is in disarray and mortal danger; yet nothing will induce it to think, to pray, to repent, or even to be honest with me. Looking in every direction but mine, it has turned against the very one who brought it up from infancy.

8:1–14 – Sowing the wind, reaping the whirlwind

When will they wake up to their danger and to my anger? How complacently they provoke me with their favourite devices – kings and gods of their own making; allies bought with promises; altars everywhere; and fortresses that will be death-traps.

9:1–17 – Wanderers among the nations

The orgy is over. What looms up now is exile. Instead of bargaining with Egypt and Assyria you will be living there – as refugees in the one, as captives in the other. What will become of your fancy religion then? And of your mockery of my prophets?

All your early promise has failed, for it was never genuine. You have always hankered after pagan gods and pagan ways. Now you must have your fill of them.

10:1–15 – 'Time to seek the Lord'

When everything went well it was pagan altars, pagan symbols everywhere. Now that all this has failed, and worse is imminent, will you listen at last? There is still a moment left, still a choice of harvests, that the Lord may come and 'shower his righteousness on you'. But the harvest you are bringing on yourselves is butchery. Assyrian butchery – you remember what that was like, last time?

11:1–11 – 'How can I give you up?'

Do you think you mean as little to me as I mean to you? I was a father to you. I taught you to walk!

But you have turned against me, and you have made up your mind. You must go through with it now: with everything that you were warned against.

Yet how can I destroy you? My love remains, and in the end my sons will come back, shaken and ashamed, home to me again.

11:12 – 12:14 – Look back and learn!

Look back now to Jacob, and see your crooked selves! But look on, too, to what God made of him when Jacob strove and wept and sought, not for advantage but for grace.

Then look at your complacent, affluent selves. You are no pilgrims! To you now only money talks – you have no ears for my prophets, who were once the making of you. You must get back to your beginnings; and if you must take your punishment you have only yourselves to blame.

13:1–16 – The unmaking of a kingdom

Once more look back. See what you were, and what you have become. See what I did for you, and how you have repaid it.

Who will extricate you now? Not I – I am the predator! Not your king – he has been taken. True, the last enemy, death, shall not have the last word; yet your city must fall, and fall to the merciless.

14:1–9 – The way home

Even now, dear Israel, turn right back to God! Attempt no payment: only seek frank forgiveness and have done with earthly substitutes for your Lord.

And his reply? 'I will heal . . . I will love . . . They shall again live beneath my shadow' (NRSV). Where sin abounded, grace will much more abound.

So to the reader: all these things are words for everyone, not just for Israel. Here is your safe path; or here, if you insist, your downfall.

The Bible Speaks Today: Old Testament series

The Message of Genesis 1 – 11
The dawn of creation
David Atkinson

The Message of Genesis 12 – 50
From Abraham to Joseph
Joyce G. Baldwin

The Message of Exodus
The days of our pilgrimage
Alec Motyer

The Message of Leviticus
Free to be holy
Derek Tidball

The Message of Numbers
Journey to the Promised Land
Raymond Brown

The Message of Deuteronomy
Not by bread alone
Raymond Brown

The Message of Joshua
Promise and people
David G. Firth

The Message of Judges
Grace abounding
Michael Wilcock

The Message of Ruth
The wings of refuge
David Atkinson

The Message of 1 and 2 Samuel
Personalities, potential, politics and power
Mary J. Evans

The Message of 1 and 2 Kings
God is present
John W. Olley

The Message of 1 and 2 Chronicles
One church, one faith, one Lord
Michael Wilcock

The Message of Ezra and Haggai
Building for God
Robert Fyall

The Message of Nehemiah
God's servant in a time of change
Raymond Brown

The Message of Esther
God present but unseen
David G. Firth

The Message of Job
Suffering and grace
David Atkinson

The Message of Psalms 1 – 72
Songs for the people of God
Michael Wilcock

The Message of Psalms 73 – 150
Songs for the people of God
Michael Wilcock

The Message of Proverbs
Wisdom for life
David Atkinson

The Message of Ecclesiastes
A time to mourn, and a time to dance
Derek Kidner

The Message of the Song of Songs
The lyrics of love
Tom Gledhill

The Message of Isaiah
On eagles' wings
Barry Webb

The Message of Jeremiah
Grace in the end
Christopher J. H. Wright

The Message of Lamentations
Honest to God
Christopher J. H. Wright

The Message of Ezekiel
A new heart and a new spirit
Christopher J. H. Wright

The Message of Daniel
His kingdom cannot fail
Dale Ralph Davis

The Message of Hosea
Love to the loveless
Derek Kidner

The Message of Joel, Micah and Habakkuk
Listening to the voice of God
David Prior

The Message of Amos
The day of the lion
Alec Motyer

The Message of Obadiah, Nahum and Zephaniah
The kindness and severity of God
Gordon Bridger

The Message of Jonah
Presence in the storm
Rosemary Nixon

The Message of Zechariah
Your kingdom come
Barry Webb

The Message of Malachi
'I have loved you,' says the Lord
Peter Adam

The Bible Speaks Today:
New Testament series

The Message of Matthew
The kingdom of heaven
Michael Green

The Message of Mark
The mystery of faith
Donald English

The Message of Luke
The Saviour of the world
Michael Wilcock

The Message of John
Here is your King!
Bruce Milne

The Message of the Sermon on the Mount (Matthew 5 – 7)
Christian counter-culture
John Stott

The Message of Acts
To the ends of the earth
John Stott

The Message of Romans
God's good news for the world
John Stott

The Message of 1 Corinthians
Life in the local church
David Prior

The Message of 2 Corinthians
Power in weakness
Paul Barnett

The Message of Galatians
Only one way
John Stott

The Message of Ephesians
God's new society
John Stott

The Message of Philippians
Jesus our joy
Alec Motyer

The Message of Colossians and Philemon
Fullness and freedom
Dick Lucas

The Message of 1 and 2 Thessalonians
Preparing for the coming King
John Stott

The Message of 1 Timothy and Titus

The life of the local church

John Stott

The Message of 2 Timothy

Guard the gospel

John Stott

The Message of Hebrews

Christ above all

Raymond Brown

The Message of James

The tests of faith

Alec Motyer

The Message of 1 Peter

The way of the cross

Edmund Clowney

The Message of 2 Peter and Jude

The promise of his coming

Dick Lucas and Chris Green

The Message of John's Letters

Living in the love of God

David Jackman

The Message of Revelation

I saw heaven opened

Michael Wilcock